I0811389

PRAISE FOR

THE NEW JERUSALEM

Before reading this book I always looked at the New Jerusalem as some future place and event. I thought how wonderful it would be if I could just live long enough to be part of it all. I now realize that the building of the New Jerusalem is happening now, and as a disciple of Jesus Christ, I have a significant role to play in that. Reading this book has renewed my faith in humanity and the goodness, strength, and beauty that can and will come as we join with the Lord in the building of His Holy City. Mostly I'm grateful for the spirit I felt as I read it and the awakening of my purpose here on earth. It was just what I needed at this time.

—JILL PIERSON, TEXAS, USA

This book is a wonderful new approach to studying the Second Coming of Jesus Christ. The author addresses the topic in a unique and fresh perspective. Rather than just a list and discussion of the signs and the times, the author addresses this topic with an emphasis on building up the New Jerusalem tied to application and preparation principles. Thoroughly researched and with an emphasis on scriptures and prophetic commentary, I felt invited to study the scriptures cited, to see for myself what they say about building up of the New Jerusalem.

—MICHAEL COTTLE, MARYLAND, USA

I have gained much knowledge about the New Jerusalem reading this book. It makes me excited for the future and what's to come. It makes me want to do my part to help gather Israel and have continued faith in Jesus Christ.

—AMBER RIGBY, UTAH USA

Building the New Jerusalem and establishing Zion are topics of supreme interest to me (and Saints at large). Ryan employs a wealth of knowledge, resources, and perspective to engage these topics and to paint a bold and beautiful picture of what we are meant to become under the direction of the Lord's anointed. Reading this book was an instructive, gratifying, and inspiring opportunity to immerse myself in the doctrine of Zion and the restoration of Israel.

—JERRY MYERS, GEORGIA, USA

This book has renewed my hope I have had for a better world. Not some unachievable utopia the world promises. It has reminded me that we need to trust in the arm of the Lord and not in the arm of the flesh.

—DARRELL FLAKE, MISSOURI, USA

I have watched Ryan Jenkins grow up. After returning from a mission for the Church, his attention became focused on learning, experiencing, and teaching about the most important elements in our lives and to gain an eternal perspective. In this book he has helped us focus on these elements, and the hope of achieving life in a Zion society.

—KEN JONES, UTAH, USA

THE NEW JERUSALEM

OTHER BOOKS BY RYAN JENKINS

- *The Assassination of Joseph Smith: Innocent Blood on the Banner of Liberty* (2015)
- *Great American Documents for Latter-day Saint Families*, Associate Editor (2012)
- *The Book of Mormon Study Guide: Start to Finish*, Associate Editor (2015)
- *The New Testament Study Guide: Start to Finish*, Associate Editor, (2018)
- *The Old Testament Study Guide: Start to Finish*, Associate Editor (2021)

OTHER PUBLICATIONS BY RYAN JENKINS

- "Peaceable Followers of Christ in Days of War and Contention," *The Religious Educator* (2009)
- "Quiet Slumber: Revelation through Dreams," *The Religious Educator* (2011)

THE NEW JERUSALEM

A HOLY CITY NOT FORSAKEN

WHAT PIECES OF THE PUZZLE DO WE HAVE?

RYAN C. JENKINS

CFI
An imprint of Cedar Fort, Inc.
Springville, Utah

ISBN 13: 978–1–4621–4126-5

Published by CFI, an imprint of Cedar Fort, Inc.
2373 W. 700 S., Springville, UT, 84663
Distributed by Cedar Fort, Inc., www.cedarfort.com

Library of Congress Control Number: 2021949112

Cover design by Courtney Proby

Printed in the United States of America

10 9 8 7 6 5 4 3 2 1

Printed on acid-free paper

In honor of those Latter-day Saints of the 1830s—
known and unknown—
who laid the foundation and bore record
of the land upon which the
Zion of God shall stand.
(D&C 58:7)

Contents

INTRODUCTION

"The vision of the New Jerusalem has moved generations of mankind. It has moved our people."[1]

I was born and reared in Las Vegas, Nevada—sin city, as many call it. Admittedly, the reasons are ubiquitously clear. You most likely have heard the cliché: "What happens in Vegas, stays in Vegas." There are probably plenty of individuals out there that hope this is true. But it is not. In confessing my place of birth, I hope it doesn't disqualify me in your mind to present ideas and themes about a forthcoming glorious city—a city that will not be a cover for sin but a pillar of righteousness for the inhabitants of the world.

What follows in this compilation has nothing to do with sensual billboards and bright lights, creative scenery, and captivating shows. What follows is the antithesis of my physical and cultural settings of which I was born and reared. Strikingly, there were many positive experiences and insights that occurred in my life during the twenty years I lived in Las Vegas, some of which may be subtly embedded in the delivery of this book.

Near my eighteenth birthday, I had the most memorable spiritual experience in my life to that point. My spiritual awakening was in two parts. Both happened at the Las Vegas Temple dedication on

1. G. Homer Durham, "The Future History of the Church," *Ensign*, May 1982.

December 16, 1989. First, President Ezra Taft Benson, with assistance, walked slowly through the front doors. He proceeded for a bit and then stopped, turned to us who were sitting in the large entry, and said, "I love you all, I love you all." Something went through me from my head to my feet. I later learned to know and appreciate what happened and who was operating upon me. Second, I became aware of remarkably clear voices that were not visibly present during the singing of the hymn "The Spirit of God."

I was stunned. I was amazed. The Lord was being very generous to me. He was giving me a chance. I knew I was not entirely right before Him at that time. If Joseph Smith could admit it, I can admit it. I needed to improve my state and standing before Him.[2] And the Savior was mercifully pulling me from the secular fires of my youth. He was presenting to me the antithesis of what was so pervasive outside the walls of His new temple. From that day, I knew there was something better. I just needed to discover it. Thirty-two years later I gladly write about, think about, and talk about a city of godliness.

Jesus Christ will reign personally upon the earth. He will establish a "holy city." He refers to this holy city as "[His] tabernacle." The holy city will also be known as, "Zion, a New Jerusalem."[3] Jesus Christ will be "her salvation and her high tower."[4] *Her salvation* may best be summed up by the gratitude expressed by king David: "The God of my rock; in him will I trust: he is my shield . . . my high tower, and my refuge, my saviour; thou savest me from violence."[5] *High tower* means "he will watch over Zion and defend her as a faithful watchman stands in his high tower to protect a city."[6]

---

2. Joseph Smith History 1:28–29.
3. See Articles of Faith 1:10; Moses 7:62.
4. D&C 97:20.
5. 2 Samuel 22:3.
6. Jay A. Parry and Donald W. Parry, *Understanding the Signs of the Times*, 178. 1999.

For these reasons, "Zion cannot fall, neither be moved out of her place, for God is there, and the hand of the Lord is there."[7] He has promised all Saints who are pure in heart and observant to His commandments will "escape" the troubles and desolations "kindled" against the wicked.[8] The Lord is in the very details. Gerald L. Lund wrote, "There is no ambiguity here. In the latter days, there will be another Zion established, a *New* Jerusalem, and it will not be [thousands of] miles away in the Old World."[9] It will be in the western hemisphere. It will be built in the center of the land "upon the American continent."[10]

The essential core truth of this compilation is to set forth that "the highest himself [Jesus Christ] shall establish her [Zion, the New Jerusalem]."[11] The earth is His footstool. His law shall go forth out of Zion. Our Righteous Father will "lay in Zion for a foundation a stone, a tried stone, a precious corner stone, a sure foundation."[12] That foundation stone, that tried stone, that precious cornerstone that provides a sure foundation is Jesus Christ. A Zion people will trust in Him. They will know without flinching He is a God unto them.[13]

The Lord has had plenty to say on this subject. Orson Pratt said, "There is no one thing more fully revealed in the Scriptures

---

7. D&C 97:19.
8. It would be helpful to study the entire 97th section of the Doctrine and Covenants. This paragraph pulls from verses 18–26.
9. Gerald Lund, *The Second Coming of the Lord*, 194.
10. Articles of Faith 1:10. See Also Ether 13:2–11.
11. Psalms 87:5. This psalm was read in its entirety on August 3, 1831 at the dedication of the temple site for the city of New Jerusalem. Joseph Smith dedicated the temple site and laid the northeast corner. Joseph had recorded: "The scene was solemn and impressive [sic]" ("History, 1838–1856, volume A-1 [23 December 1805–30 August 1834],"139; *The Joseph Smith Papers*, accessed September 1, 2020, https://www.josephsmithpapers.org/paper-summary/history-1838-1856-volume-a-1-23-december-1805-30-august-1834/145).
12. Isaiah 28:16. See also 1 Peter 2:6-8.
13. See Genesis 17:7 and Exodus 6:7.

of eternal truth, than the rise of the Zion of our God in the latter days, clothed upon with the glory of God from the heavens."[14] Satan knows this. The wicked one is, without cessation, destroying cities with fear and gross wickedness. This is causing the earth and her feign kingdoms to tremble and shake.[15] The thought of the Lord countering his works with a holy people gathering to build and sustain a holy city must enrage him. And we have scriptural accounts that describe his behavior when he is enraged.

A few commentators have observed: "It is interesting to note that the first recorded instance in the Doctrine and Covenants of false revelation in this dispensation dealt with the upbuilding of Zion. Satan attempted to mislead Saints in their understanding of this important work of the Lord."[16] In September 1830, only a few months after the organization of the Church, Hiram Page was claiming to receive revelations concerning Zion. "Among the things he attempted to make known was where this city was to be built."[17] He was corrected and taught the Lord's order of establishing Zion. Hiram was to be told matter-of-factly, "Satan [had deceived] him."[18]

To be warned and to learn caution ourselves, we ought to consider Hiram Page's account on a personal level. The Lord has a pattern and has given appointment to His presiding key holders. Therefore, I am not trying to present sensational material. I am not trying to rally people to a cause. I am trying to present the scriptural and prophetic foundation of the theme at hand. In the preface to his book *The Second Coming of the Lord,* Gerald Lund stated that his compilation "represents my own interpretations of the scriptures and the words of our prophets. . . . I see this book as a *joint exploration*

---

14. Orson Pratt, *Journal of Discourses*, 16:78.
15. Isaiah foresaw this. Consider his words on Lucifer in Isaiah 14:12–17.
16. Leaun G. Otten and C. Max Caldwell, *Sacred Truths of the Doctrine and Covenants*, 1:276.
17. *Doctrines of Salvation* 3:75.
18. See D&C 28.

between author and reader, not a collection of infallible declarations and conclusions."[19] His statement reflects my heart and desires.

I hope you enjoy exploring. I hope you have several questions, ideas, and inspired thoughts that you can anchor in scripture and modern-day prophets. Remember, as Elder D. Todd Christofferson testified, "The Church of Jesus Christ of Latter-day Saints is uniquely empowered and commissioned to accomplish the necessary preparations for the Lord's Second Coming." He added, "This great and last dispensation is building steadily to its climax—Zion on earth being joined with Zion from above at the Savior's glorious return."[20] After the building of the city and the gathering has occurred the Lord has put on record, "then shall the power of heaven come down among them; and I also will be in the midst."[21]

Hasten the day.

—Ryan Jenkins
2021

---

19. See preface of *The Second Coming of the Lord*, xvi (Deseret Book, 2020).
20. D. Todd Christofferson "Preparing for the Lord's Return," *Ensign*, May 2019.
21. 3 Nephi 21:25.

1

Emma Smith and Our Inheritance in Zion

"I desire the Spirit of God to know and understand myself, that I might be able to overcome whatever of tradition or nature that would not tend to my exaltation."[1]

In a book about a holy city to be prepared and built up by the Lord and His people in the last days, why would I draw attention to Emma Hale Smith?

According to an early revelation in the Church (see D&C 25), Emma Smith was the first person promised by the Lord that she would receive an inheritance in Zion. And, the revelation she received (which was shortly after her baptism) is the Lord's "voice unto all."[2] This was emphasized poignantly for me one day from the following experience.

The first time my wife and I met the family of our daughter-in-law, Katie, we witnessed a tender interchange. Katie has a large

1. Emma Smith, *Daughters in My Kingdom*, 12.
2. D&C 25:16.

family. The day of this interchange had many of them present. We were in the backyard of her sister's home. After dinner, Grandpa and Grandma (Katie's parents) called everyone around. The grandchildren and nearly all the adults gathered. Imagine a football team gathering on the sideline just before going onto the field. This is what the gathering looked like.

Grandpa and Grandma were in the middle being surrounded by their posterity. Like a sports team, there was hype and excitement. Arms were around each other, movement up down. Everyone knew what was coming. It wasn't rehearsed, but it was a rich part of their large family gatherings. As the huddle became more cohesive and intimate, the grandparents led everyone in a recitation.

It caught me by surprise. All joined in saying, "Wherefore, lift up thy heart and rejoice, and cleave unto the covenants which thou hast made."[3]

I was taken aback by the powerful feeling that overcame me. I instantly fell in love with these people. The words "cleave unto the covenants which thou hast made" reverberated in my mind. I knew the language was from the Doctrine and Covenants. I pulled out my phone to confirm it was a revelation given to Emma Smith. This revelation, and with Emma Smith, is where I want to spend a few paragraphs with you.

Harmony Township, Pennsylvania, now called Oakland, is the birthplace of Emma Hale Smith. This region in southern Pennsylvania has beautiful hills and valleys. It was here that Emma Hale flourished into a radiant young adult. It was here that her kind, yet resilient nature developed. She was born into an industrious home with responsible parents.[4] Her spiritual, emotional, mental, and physical strength matured in such a way that prepared her to marry a unique man.

---

3. Long live the Frank and Ginny Judd Family. This experience happened in June of 2018. D&C 25:13.
4. Daughter of Isaac Hale and Elizabeth Lewis. Member of Methodist church at Harmony (later in Oakland). See *JSP Website, People.* Emma Smith.

On January 18, 1827, Emma Hale married Joseph Smith, a man whom the Lord was tutoring and preparing to restore truth and authority that would extend the blessings of exaltation to all our Father in Heaven's children. Through appointed messengers, Jesus Christ would bestow the keys of the priesthood upon Joseph Smith, which granted the right and responsibility to set forth the ordinances of exaltation. In June of 1830, Emma would enter the waters of baptism, the first significant ordinance leading to exaltation.[5] At this point in her life she had now accepted two significant ordinances required for exaltation—baptism and marriage. Both baptism and marriage were clearly taught by the Savior.[6] A higher order of the marriage covenant through ordinance would be received by them in 1843.[7]

It was also at this time that she began to claim a promise the Savior issued during His mortal ministry: "And every one that hath forsaken houses, or brethren, or sisters, or father, or mother, or wife, or children, or lands for my name's sake, shall receive an hundredfold, and shall inherit everlasting life."[8]

What did Emma forsake? In a rather short amount of time after she was married to Joseph, Emma Smith had financial difficulties and persecution thrust upon her. She would forsake all eight elements mentioned by the Savior in the above verse. Upon leaving Pennsylvania she would never see her parents again. "After moving, she never returned to the Susquehanna, and her parents seem to have cut off contact with her until after her father's death in 1839."[9] She would

---

5. Matthew 3:13–17; 7:13–14.
6. See John 3:3–7 and Matthew 19:3–8.
7. May 28, 1843. Joseph and Emma were sealed under the power of the holy priesthood (*BYU Studies*, Vol. 46, No.4, 148).
8. Matthew 19:29. See also Matthew 10:34–38.
9. Mark L. Staker and Curtis Ashton, "Emma's Susquehanna: Growing Up in the Isaac and Elizabeth Hale Home," August 25, 2015. Priesthood Restoration Site, churchofjesuschrist.org. Additionally, the words of the Savior might be considered here: "For I am come to set a man at variance against his father, and the daughter against her mother, and the daughter in law against her mother in law" (Matthew 10:35).

see some of her siblings again, but not all. Within fourteen years she would forsake numerous homes and lands for the gospel's sake. She buried several children, some of which may have lived if persecution hadn't been thrust upon them. She also buried her husband after seventeen years of marriage, a husband who was killed in cold blood giving his life to the Savior and His restored Church.

Though conflicted for a time, Emma stayed "virtuous and pure" before the Lord in her marriage covenant."[10] The Lord exhorted her to "abide and cleave" unto Joseph in the new and everlasting covenant of marriage, which included plural marriage. Without breaking her marriage covenant she fought through her feelings and objections to the institution of this doctrine until the death of her husband. [11]

In His exhortation, the Lord encouraged Emma to "forgive" Joseph his trespasses, with the promise that if she did, she would be forgiven. She was also promised that the Lord would personally "bless her, and multiply her, and make her heart rejoice."[12] In the revelation on plural marriage, and at the deepest anguish she may have been passing through, the Lord refers to her as His "handmaid."[13] This is a respectful term. One author summarizes the title: "A handmaid is a personal female servant. In the same sense in which John the Baptist referred to Joseph Smith and Oliver Cowdery as his 'fellow servants' in the ministry of the Messiah (D&C 13:1), women who so serve are often referred to as handmaidens."[14] This is something

---

10. D&C 132:52.
11. D&C 132:54. The language in this revelation should be carefully studied. For example, when the word "destroyed" is used it may be best to consider the idea "cut off" or "destroyed among the people." See Acts 3:23. Emma was severed from the body of the Saints. It is indisputable that she chose to cut herself off from the association of the Saints moving west. However, The Lord or His servants never had her excommunicated. Also, in some respects her name has been destroyed by the ignorance and miscalculations of people up to this day.
12. D&C 132:56.
13. D&C 132:51, 54, 56, for example.
14. Hoyt W. Brewster, *Doctrine and Covenants Encyclopedia*, 229.

to keep in mind, as some cast judgment or mischaracterize this significant Latter-day Saint.[15]

The Lord told Emma to "lay aside the things of this world.[16]" In many instances she didn't have to lay them aside—they were taken from her by the hands of wicked people. In many instances, her sufferings subdued any clamoring over the vanity of the world. She responded favorably to the calls and plight of other individuals. A quality or trait those caught up in the world have no interest in. For these reasons it is not surprising that in modern revelation, Emma Smith was the first person promised an inheritance in Zion.[17]

There is no evidence this grand promise to Emma was ever revoked. Her diligence may prove to swallow up any personal blemishes. If repentance is granted to us, it has surely been granted to her. She will once again enjoy beautiful hills and valleys like unto her birthplace.[18] Her inheritance in Zion will be glorious. Her heart will rejoice. When Joseph Smith Sr. blessed her in December of 1834 he stated: "Thou shall see many days; yea, the Lord will spare thee till thou art satisfied, for thou shalt see thy Redeemer. Thy heart shall rejoice in the great work of the Lord, and no one shall take thy rejoicing from thee."[19]

---

15. Wilford Woodruff felt to dignify her in 1892 when women of the Relief Society were celebrating fifty years of their organization through jubilee. Portraits of Emma and Joseph were going to be hung in the tabernacle as part of the celebration. Some took umbrage because Emma did not come west and had joined her sons Reorganized Church of Jesus Christ of Latter-day Saints. Zina Young asked President Woodruff what he thought about the debate. He matter-of-factly stated, "Anyone who opposes it, must be very narrow-minded indeed." Few living new Emma and her situation as good or better than Wilford Woodruff. See *Saints: No Unhallowed Hand* (vol. 2), The Church of Jesus Christ of Latter-day Saints, 2020, 632.
16. D&C 25:10.
17. D&C 25:2.
18. See D&C 35:24: 39:13.
19. "Blessing from Joseph Smith Sr., 9 December 1834," *The Joseph Smith Papers*, 4, accessed January 19, 2021, https://www.josephsmithpapers.org/paper-summary/blessing-from-joseph-smith-sr-9-december-1834/2.

Shouldn't we be interested in the counsel of the Lord to an individual who was promised an inheritance in Zion? For us to accomplish the buildup of Zion we will need spiritual, emotional, mental, and physical strength as exemplified in Emma Hale Smith. Doctrine and Covenants 25 lays out what we will need to do. We will need to "lay aside the things of this world." We are going to have to choose faithfulness and "walk in the paths of virtue." We are going to have to choose, or as the Lord said, "seek for things of a better." For us to build up Zion we will have to "lift up [our] heart[s] and rejoice, and cleave unto the covenants which [we] have made." We must "beware of pride."[20] We must be alert and discerning.

And as Brigham Young taught, we must not only forsake many things and perhaps family and friends for the Lord's cause, but we must also work a change personally. "Many Latter-day Saints think when they have obeyed the Gospel, made a sacrifice in forsaking their homes, perhaps their parents, husbands, wives, children, farms, native lands, or other things held dear, that the work is done; but it is only just commenced. The work of purifying ourselves and preparing to build up the Zion of God . . . has only just begun."[21]

A unique work will require a ready people with remarkable hearts and willing minds to accomplish things that may have never been thought of.[22] A marvelous work and a wonder requires marvelous people. Emma Hale Smith provided a fine example. Again, we ought to accept the fact that if repentance is granted to us it surely is granted to her. The revelation given to her (now known as D&C 25) should be very familiar to us, something to know and remember as we push forward to understand and to establish Zion, the New Jerusalem, the Holy City.

On October 29, 1835, Emma Smith hosted a large dinner party. Edward Partridge, the bishop of Zion, was visiting Kirtland, Ohio. At dinner, Newel K. Whitney, a bishop in Kirtland, "told Edward

---

20. Again, I draw attention to the whole section of D&C 25.
21. *Discourses of Brigham Young*, 444.
22. See D&C 64:34.

that he hoped to dine with him the next year in Zion." The remark influenced Emma. Turning to her friends at the dinner she said she hoped everyone at the table might be able to join them in the promised land as well.[23]

Imagine yourself at that dinner table. She was speaking to you. She was speaking to me. She was on the front end of the buildup of Zion. We are approaching the back end of the buildup of Zion. I look forward to the day when we join each other in the promised land of Zion, the New Jerusalem.

23. *Saints: [The Standard of Truth]*, Vol. 1:222–223.

2

Where Is the New Jerusalem?

"The decree hath gone forth from the Father they shall be gathered in unto one place upon the face of this land."[1]

Have you looked at a map of the United States recently? Pull one up on your device or reach for your Rand McNally road atlas. Refresh and reset your mind to eighth-grade geography. Near Lebanon Kansas, about 2.5 miles to the northwest, is a marker, a monument. It designates the geographic center of the continental United States. It is not far from the geography discussed in this chapter. I don't want to focus on Lebanon, Kansas, but rather on the concept of the center of the land, or the "center place" the Lord identifies in revelation.

Many religious settlers in the Americas of the seventeenth and eighteenth centuries believed in a Zion concept. Many believed in a New Jerusalem concept and strongly felt the western hemisphere was the place. Additionally, many believed it was toward the center of the land mass or continent. They were not alone. Other people in previous generations had known and believed in a glorious city to be built in the last days. Joseph Smith was not introducing a new

1. D&C 29:8 (September 1830).

concept that was foreign to alert and discerning Bible readers. He was amplifying it.

The prophecies are numerous.[2] A modern-day seer would develop the reality of a New Jerusalem. The Lord would begin revealing components of a future city to be built. There will be a physical gathering. The City of Zion, the New Jerusalem, will be built. Joseph Smith said, "Prophets, priests, and kings have dwelt with peculiar delight; they have looked forward with joyful anticipation."[3] Righteous men and women today and of past ages have a profound interest and involvement in the undertaking.

Ancient and modern prophets were and are sure of its place. American soil has been designated.[4] Western Missouri has been identified by the Lord for the foundation of the city. Missouri has a storied past, a quiet present, and a delightful future. From a holy garden to a holy city, the region has been under the Lord's direct care for thousands of years.[5] I suppose we can expect more knowledge on this region's beginnings and its future development as events unfold.

---

2. One of the purposes of this compilation is to bring attention to the prophecies in the Old Testament, New Testament, Book of Mormon, Doctrine and Covenants, and the Pearl of Great Price. Also statements from modern prophets.
3. Joseph Smith statement. See "History, 1838–1856, volume C-1 [2 November 1838–31 July 1842]," *The Joseph Smith Papers*, 137, accessed June 16, 2020, https://www.josephsmithpapers.org/paper-summary/history-1838-1856-volume-c-1-2-november-1838-31-july-1842/501
4. Most recently, in the April 2020 *Ensign*, President Russell M. Nelson confirmed the building of the New Jerusalem will be built upon the American continent.
5. "It is a pleasant thing to think of and to know where the garden of Eden was. . . . In Jackson County was the garden of Eden. Joseph has declared this and I am as much bound to believe that as to believe Joseph was a prophet of God" (*Journal History* of The Church of Jesus Christ of Latter-day Saints, March 15, 1857, Church History Library, 1). In 1873 Wilford Woodruff would declare that Brigham Young had taught the people that Joseph Smith told him that the Garden of Eden was in Jackson Co., Missouri" (*Wilford Woodruff Journal*, March 30 1873, Church History Library).

At present, we must confront man's designation marks of the land. On a boundary map, Missouri has a distinct shape. That is to be expected when the eastern border is defined by the Mississippi River and nearly half of the western border is defined by the Missouri River. Missouri has many neighbors and borders eight different states.[6] But, the Lord's purposes and plans are not limited to man's designated boundaries. Western Missouri, particularly Jackson County, is a starting point for Zion, the New Jerusalem. The term "land of Zion" is used seventy times in the Doctrine and Covenants. The term "land of Missouri" is used nine times. They are used interchangeably.

The revelations dictate the "purchasing of all the lands in Jackson county that can be purchased, and in the adjoining counties round about."[7] The Lord uses directions and places in the revelations to help mortal man comprehend His own divine designations. We should not be overly zealous with an X-marks-the-spot approach. Man's boundaries are temporary and often subject to change. For example, today's Jackson County doesn't resemble what it looked like when the Lord began giving Joseph Smith revelations about the "land of Missouri" or the "region." Today's Jackson County is one-third the size it was in 1831 when the revelation "for the city of Zion" was received.[8]

In Joseph Smiths' day, all of Jackson and Cass Counties and parts of Bates County were considered Jackson County. This is something to keep in mind as we consider geography and gathering. To emphasize this point even more, where there were four counties in western Missouri in Joseph Smith's time, there are nineteen counties today. Today, more than twenty-five counties represent those immediate "counties round about" (see map at the end of this chapter).

And what about the region westward into modern-day Kansas (Wyandotte, Johnson, and Miami Counties)? What about Lebanon,

---

6. For "geography junkies" those states include Kansas, Oklahoma, Arkansas, Tennessee, Kentucky, Illinois, Iowa, and Nebraska. Tennessee is the only other state that has eight neighbors.
7. D&C 105:28.
8. D&C 57:1–2, 6. Note "land of" and "region" as stated in the revelation.

Kansas, to the west of Jackson County and Missouri? Is it part of this region? In referencing a return to the Midwest to build up Zion, Orson Pratt thought broadly on the geography. He declared in 1879 at a conference of the Church in Salt Lake City: "Not many years hence . . . you will look forth to the western counties of the State of Missouri, and to the eastern counties of the State of Kansas, and in all the region round about."[9] Again, we must be cautious in trying to designate boundaries with regards to the city of Zion. We don't know how big the city (or cities/communities) will be. The Lord has not revealed it.[10] Consider the first designating revelation on the City of Zion:

> Hearken, O ye elders of my church, saith the Lord your God, who have assembled yourselves together, according to my commandments, in this land, which is *the land of Missouri*, which is *the land* which I have appointed and consecrated for the gathering of the Saints.
>
> Wherefore, this is *the land of promise*, and *the place for the city of Zion*.
>
> And thus saith the Lord your God, if you will receive wisdom here is wisdom. Behold, the place which is now called *Independence is the center place*; and *a spot* for the temple is lying westward, upon a lot which is not far from the courthouse. Wherefore, it is wisdom that *the land* should be purchased by the Saints, and also *every tract lying westward*, even unto *the line running directly between Jew and Gentile*.[11]

In this revelation, the Lord designates the land, the center place, and the spot. That center place and spot are in context of the

---

9. *Journal of Discourses* 21:135.
10. The New Jerusalem, which will descend from heaven above (see Revelation 21:16–17), may be 1500 miles square (12,000 furlongs). This will take a nice piece of land. How this all interlays with the Zion built by the Saints, or if it is one in the same, is not entirely understood by me.
11. D&C 57:1–4; emphasis added.

temple.[12] But to build a city requires land, and lots of it. In just a few short words the Lord referred to "the land" four times. The "line running directly between Jew and Gentile" refers to the western boundary of the United States at the time. Missouri officially became a state in 1821. Kansas obtained statehood in 1861. The revelation quoted above was received in 1831. The United States had constantly changing policies regarding Indians and their removal to western lands. Joseph Fielding Smith observed that this distinct statement by the Lord had reference to "the line separating the Lamanites from the settlers in Jackson County. . . . The Lamanites, who are Israelites, were referred to as Jews, and the Gentiles were the people many of whom were of the lawless element, living east of the river."[13]

At the time, Saints would not

The Land. Sidney Rigdon "consecrated and dedicated" the land of Zion (the region and surrounding counties) on August 2, 1831. This took place 12 miles west of Independence, in Kaw Township.

The Center Place. Joseph Smith arrived in Independence Missouri, July 14, 1831. This was his first visit to western Missouri. Independence was declared the "center place" on July 20, 1831.

The Spot. The temple site was designated July 20, 1831 by revelation. It was dedicated on August 3, 1831 by Joseph Smith. "The 87th Psalm was read. . . . The Scene was solemn and impressive."

---

12. D&C 84:1–5 addresses this more.
13. *Church History and Modern Revelation*, vol. 1:189. See also footnote b for D&C 57:4. Online. See *Revelations in Context,* 122–127. The Center Place: D&C 52, 57, 58. (Jed Woodworth) has written in this chapter: "Doctrine and Covenants 57 observed the existence of this settlement line without endorsing it. The revelation noted that Zion should be built along "the line running directly between Jew and Gentile," or the line separating the state of Missouri from Indian Territory to the west. The revelation resisted the usual categories, however, primarily through its curious use of the terms Jew and Gentile. The standard terms then used by Americans—white and Indian or white and red—suggested a racial and cultural divide. The two groups were worlds apart, and white people often deployed the terminology to emphasize this incompatibility."

have been able to purchase land in Indian territory (Kansas). A reason, perhaps, that the Lord made the distinction in the revelation. But that distinction cannot be definitive. He could and most likely will have more land as the city of Zion unfolds. Church agents have bought and sold land in and around this region of Missouri and Kansas for years. If the center place is what we call Independence, Missouri, in our day (and Joseph Smith's day), then we ought to expect that the circumference will reach both north, east, south, and west (don't lose hope, people of Lebanon, Kansas).

It should be remembered that sacred land lies to the north. A land where former people lived in joy, suffered untold persecution, and gathered for protection as well as for an endowment of power. It was a land where the Lord's people were driven and scattered by an evil power.[14] For example, Far West, Missouri, is fifty miles north of Independence, the center place. In the spring of 1838, the Lord stated: "It is my will that the city of Far West should be built up speedily by the gathering of my Saints. And also *other places* should be appointed for stakes *in the regions round about*."[15] Today, the designated spot and area of Far West is uniquely quiet and scarcely populated. The Lord can "make solitary places to bud and to blossom and to bring forth in abundance."[16]

Another example, Adam-Ondi-Ahman, is eighty miles *north* of the center place. This creates a very interesting radius from the center place. This is especially true as we consider the words of the psalmists who declared that the north side of Zion ("the city of our God") would be beautifully situated (elevated) and the joy of whole earth.[17] Some points of interest may be helpful or simply something to consider. First, "there was in various lands a concept that the dwelling

---

14. D&C 107:53–56 gives us a time of endowment of power in the days of aging Father Adam.
15. D&C 115:17–18; italics for emphasis.
16. D&C 117:7.
17. Psalm 48:1–3.

place of Deity was in the 'north.'"[18] Second, when Isaiah described Lucifer's pre-earth rant we learn: "I will ascend into heaven, I will exalt my throne above the stars of God." He didn't stop there. He would declare that he would "sit also upon the mount of the congregation, in the sides of the north" where Deity was known to dwell.[19] Third, Adam-ondi-Ahman may mean "the place or land of God where Adam dwelt."[20] Adam met with the Gods there at least once. He will meet them there again.

---

18. Ibid. See footnote d for Psalm 48:2 in the LDS King James Version of the Bible.
19. Isaiah 14:13; italics for emphasis. From a periodical published in Joseph Smith's day (Nauvoo time period) we get some views on how their day viewed Psalm 48:1–3: "David evidently saw the situation of Zion, which he says is beautiful, at some other place besides Jerusalem, or he would not have said that it was on the sides of the North. Match this saying with what Isaiah says in (chapter 18) of his prophecy, concerning a land [America] beyond the rivers of Ethiopia, and we learn: first, as Isaiah says, that this is the land where the Lord's ensign of the last days was to be reared, and from whence the ambassadors of the Lord are to be sent to all nations, and where "the place of the name of the Lord of hosts, the Mount Zion" shall be established, to which the servants of God, or swift messengers to the nations shall bring a present unto the Lord of a people terrible from their beginning.—This proves that Zion is to be located in America. Second, that, according to David, it is to be on the sides of the North; consequently, on North America. David says in another place: "I will not give sleep to my eyes nor slumber to mine eyelids until I find out a place for the Lord, an habitation for the mighty God of Jacob. Lo, we heard of it at Ephrata; we found it in the fields of the wood." "For the Lord hath chosen Zion: he hath desired it for his habitation."—(Ps. 132: 4,13). It cannot be said in truth that Jerusalem was in the fields of the wood in David's time; therefore, we conclude that he had reference to some other place besides Jerusalem. Indeed, the interior of North America is interspersed with the fields of the woods, or in other words fields in the midst of the wilderness. Isaiah says: "Zion is a wilderness, Jerusalem a desolation" (*Times and Seasons,* vol. 2 [Salt Lake City: Deseret Book, 2020], 475).
20. Robert J. Matthews, "Adam-ondi-Ahman," *BYU Studies*, vol. 13, no. 1 (1972): 27–35.

Satan wants to thwart our inheritance in Zion, the city of God. He may even be clamoring for a significant seat when Adam-ondi-Ahman (a place and a gathering) is held. He desires to exalt himself. The vagabond is miserably roaming up and down the earth.[21] He knows the past. He knows the sacred lands. He knows where righteous Saints will be gathered in the last days. "By revealing the location of Adam-ondi-Ahman to Joseph Smith, the Lord imbued the land in Daviess County with a spiritual history as well as a spiritual future."[22] The evil one wants a part in it. He ranted about it long ago. Thankfully, he will be subdued.

When you consider other potential radiuses to the east, south, and west, we start to envision the grandeur of the prophecies and wonderful possibilities of gathering.

It should be remembered that earlier Saints of this dispensation did settle in Far West and Adam-Ondi-Ahman. These earlier Saints were foundation contractors. They literally and symbolically set cornerstones for cities, temples, churches, schools, quorums, and organizations, for families then, and in the future. "At the time of Joseph Smith's arrival in 1838, Far West had a population of 4,900."[23] There were about 150 homes and a select number commerce establishments to sustain the growing population. Likewise, in the fall of 1838, Adam-ondi-Ahman had "upwards of two hundred houses" and about "forty families living in their wagons."[24] This is not the visible setting today. Beautiful, open land awaits a better day. Under the direction of the First Presidency and the Presiding Bishopric, the Lord is, and will, do His work in reclaiming these sacred lands.

---

21. Job 1:7.
22. *Revelations in Context: The Stories behind the Sections of the Doctrine and Covenants*, 238 [chapter written by Jacob W. Olmstead]. Published by The Church of Jesus Christ of Latter-day Saints, 2016. Edited by Matthew McBride and James Goldberg.
23. Ibid.
24. Ibid. See pages 236 and 239, particularly. For more context it is suggested that a reader review pages 235–240.

The Lord has His land designated. "And, behold, there is none other place appointed than that which I have appointed; neither shall there be any other place appointed than that which I have appointed, for the work of the gathering of my Saints."[25]

The Lord knows what He needs. He can set His own geographical boundaries to a city of holiness. He can designate His own stakes of Zion. Gratefully He has given us, in His wisdom, a geographical foundation. More important, He has revealed "a spot" for the temple. What is a holy city without holy temples? With a temple and temples occupying designated spots in this region and throughout the world the Lord will be able to build up and gather His Saints into geographical havens—the city of New Jerusalem and her stakes.

1830 Missouri County Boundaries

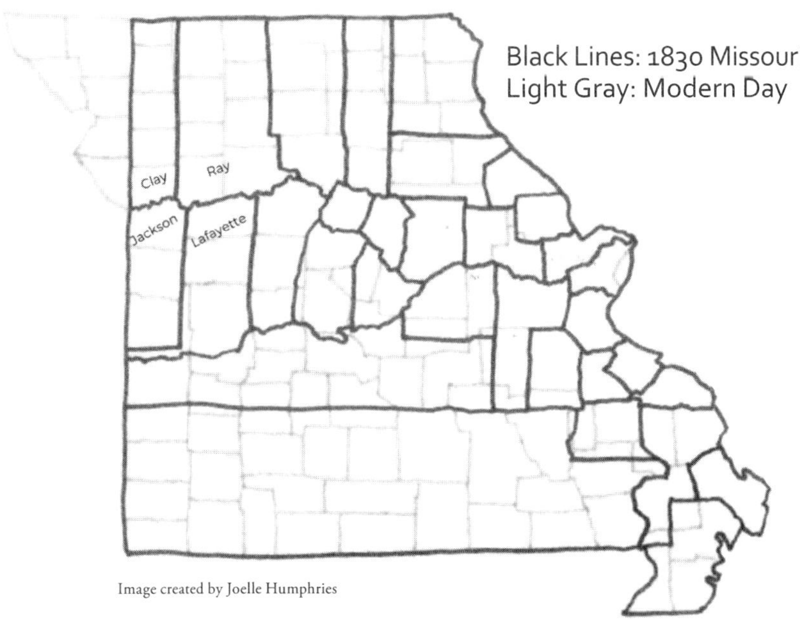

Image created by Joelle Humphries

25. D&C 101:20.

3

The City of New Jerusalem—How and When

"In regard to the building up of Zion, it has to be done by the counsel of Jehovah, by the revelations of heaven."[1]

Be careful of "every Tom, Dick or Harry." An idiom that is documented to be well over three hundred years old relates to everyone or anyone who falls short of significance or authority. (No offense if your legal name is Tom, Dick, or Harry.)

I must start with attention to this phrase to set up what President Harold B. Lee said about gathering to western Missouri. "When the Lord gets ready . . . He will direct us through the proper channels; He won't do it through some Tom, Dick, or Harry who gets an idea he's going to buy lands and therefore call the people back to build up Jackson County. I think it is important to keep that in mind.

1. *Teachings of Presidents of the Church: Joseph Smith*, 186.

The time will be when the Lord tells us."[2] What are those proper channels in which the Lord will direct us? How can you understand and give significant attention to those proper channels? One way is to understand what the Lord revealed to His seer Joseph Smith. During his first visit to Jackson County, Missouri, Joseph received a revelation on the subject and question at hand.

> For, behold, verily I say unto you, the Lord willeth that the disciples and the children of men should open their hearts, even to purchase this whole region of country, as soon as time will permit. Behold, here is wisdom. Let them do this lest they receive none inheritance, save it be by the shedding of blood. And again, inasmuch as there is land obtained, let there be workmen sent forth of all kinds unto this land, to labor for the Saints of God. Let all these things be done in order; and let the privileges of the lands be made known from time to time, by the bishop or the agent of the church. And let the work of the gathering be not in haste, nor by flight; but let it be done as it shall be counseled by the elders of the church at the conferences, according to the knowledge which they receive from time to time.[3]

---

2. Harold B. Lee, *The Teachings of Harold B. Lee.* 1996, 526. Coincidentally another president of the Church was fond of this idiom. Joseph F. Smith emphasized: "And I know this, that God has organized his Church in the earth, and I know that when he designs or purposes to make any change in the matter of governing or controlling or presiding over the affairs of his Church, that he will make the change, and he will make it in such a way that the whole people of the Church, who are doing right, will understand and accept it. I know that the Lord will not raise up 'Tom, Dick, or Harry,' here, there and everywhere, claiming to be Christ, or 'one mighty and strong,' claiming to be inspired and called to do some wonderful thing. The Lord will not deal with men in that way; that while the organization of the Church exists, while quorums and councils of the Priesthood are intact in the Church, the Lord will reveal his purposes through them, and not through 'Tom, Dick, or Harry.' Put that in your little note books now, and remember it; it is true" (John A. Widtsoe, *Gospel Doctrine, Selections from the Sermons and Writings of Joseph F. Smith*, 36).
3. D&C 58:52–56.

As the early Latter-day Saints began to move to Missouri, they were encouraged to do so in wisdom, order, and under the counsel of Church leaders.[4] They were to purchase property through legal processes. Today, land is owned by the Church and by members independently. An important thing to remember is the Lord will render unto Caesar the things which are Caesar's.[5] This idea of purchasing and negotiating land may be ongoing for quite some time. It has been happening and is currently happening under the direction of the presiding councils of the Church.[6]

It is also of interest to note from this revelation that "workmen" of "all kinds" will be "sent." Who these workmen are or when they will go has not been designated. Could they be workmen of all kinds of persuasions? Why not? There is plenty of skill and knowledge out there of like-minded people who can unite their efforts with and "for the Saints of God." Regardless, they will be sent. The flow of the revelation confirms all things "will be done in order."

The designated agent of the Church is the president of the Church. He is flanked by other prophets, seers, and revelators, as well as the presiding bishopric. The presiding bishopric oversee the temporal work of the Church. The idea that they (the prophets) will receive knowledge "from time to time" should remind us the Lord has not given living prophets all knowledge concerning the New Jerusalem. It will come with His wisdom and will be done in order. It will come forth by way of those who have designated priesthood keys.

---

4. See *Saints Vol. 1*: 156–157 for an early dispensational example. William McLellin and others put a strain on the resources and overwhelmed Bishop Partridge.
5. D&C 63:26. Verses 27–31 also provide important context on why purchasing the land is vital.
6. In 1995, President Gordon B. Hinckley was asked by an investigative journalist, Mike Wallace, about the 3,000 acres the Church owns in western Missouri and Jesus's return to there. President Hinckley told him he would rather not talk about that. "The point misses the point," he said.

Elder Graham Doxey (1927–2013) once stated: "Scripture makes it clear that Missouri has a prophetic role to play in the Second Coming and it seems logical that some people will need to go there to assist in portions of that work. But the scriptures contain no references that spell out in detail how that assistance will be given."[7] Therefore, it is a great blessing to have modern prophets who can receive instruction on how to call forth and set forth that assistance. In 1849, Elder Orson Pratt, a foundational Saint of this dispensation conveyed his feelings:

> If the building up of the city of Zion must assuredly take place before the Lord appears in his glory, then there must assuredly be more revelation given to accomplish so important a work. No uninspired man would know when to commence such a work; neither would he know the place where the Most High would have such a city; neither would he know anything of the order of architecture which would be the most pleasing in the sight of Jehovah; neither would he know anything of the size or pattern of the sanctuary and tabernacle which, according to the scriptures, must be built in Zion. An uninspired man would be in total ignorance in regard to everything connected with this preparatory city for the coming of the Lord. Hence the great necessity for more revelation and inspired prophets in the last days.[8]

As the world conditions spiral out of control, we may become impatient with the timing and pace. I suppose many want to see hard evidence. They want to see gathering Saints, temples and other buildings being constructed. They want to see enemies to Jesus Christ subdued. And a host of other evidence. The adversary gets the advantage of us when we make decisions or act with impatience or impulsiveness. There is plenty of work to do where we are now in our current homes, towns, cities, states, providences, and nations.

---

7. "Missouri Myths," *Ensign*, April 1979.
8. Orson Pratt, *New Jerusalem or the Fulfillment of Modern Prophecy*. (Liverpool, England, October 1, 1849), 39.

In the same revelation (D&C 58) I quoted a few paragraphs ago, we also get this gem. "Concerning the elders of the church, the time has not yet come, *for many years*, for them to receive their inheritance in this land." Why? Where were the elders and Saints and their families to live and what were they to do? The same which we are being commanded and strongly encouraged to do today, "push people together from the ends of the earth."[9]

> "Continuing revelation is the means by which the Lord administers His timing. We need that revelatory direction. For example, many of us or our descendants will doubtless participate in the fulfillment of prophecies about the building of the city of New Jerusalem (see D&C 84:2–4). But in this matter the timing is the Lord's, not ours. We will not be approved or blessed in clearing the ground or pouring the footings for that great project until the Lord has said that it is time. In this, as in so many other things, the Lord will proceed in His own time and in His own way."
>
> —Dallin H. Oaks
>
> ("Timing," BYU Speeches, January 29, 2002).

"Push people together from the ends of the earth." What a hidden phrase in scripture! To me, it's another way to say, go to the four corners of the earth and gather Israel. This is what the Lord needs us to be doing in earnest. This is what modern prophets are unflinchingly teaching and inspiring today. The glory that will rest upon Zion, the New Jerusalem, and her complementing stakes throughout the world depends on our current efforts to "push people together." Ultimately, "that in the dispensation of the fulness of times he (God the Father) might gather together in one all things in [Jesus] Christ, both which are in heaven, and which are on earth; even in him."[10]

9. D&C 58:44–45. Note the "for many years" language.

10. Ephesians 1:10.

It has been nearly two hundred years since the Lord gave the parable of the nobleman. In the parable He describes what inhibited foundational Saints to build up the city of New Jerusalem.[11] It also gives insights to what the Lord needs to accumulate to do this work in preparing for the New Jerusalem. In the revelation the Lord says, "By and by I may come with the residue of mine house and possess the land." In the parable the Lord's servant (Joseph Smith, see D&C 103:21) asks, "When shall these things be?" The answer is vague but sure: "When I will." Adding, "After many days."[12]

That's not much to go on for impatient people who live hour to hour, day to day, week by week, month to month, and year to year. Elder Bruce R. McConkie explained the when and how of the New Jerusalem this way:

> As we are aware, the building of the New Jerusalem lies in the future, at a time yet to be designated by revelation. There is no present call for the Saints to purchase land or to live in Jackson County or in any place connected therewith. The revealed word relative to the gathering to Independence and its environs will come through the prophet of God on earth. When it does come—with the consequent return of the Saints to that Zion which shall not be moved out of its place—that call will not be for the Saints in general to assemble there. The return to Jackson County will be by delegates, as it were. Those whose services are needed there will assemble as appointed. The rest of Israel will remain in their appointed places. The Lord's house is a house of order, and faithful Saints do as they are told and go at the bidding of their prophet, for his voice is the voice of the Lord. And as

11. Read and ponder the parable of the nobleman and the redemption of Zion in D&C 101:43–62.
12. D&C 101:58–62. The Lord has also stated: "Behold, the land of Zion—I, the Lord, hold it in mine own hands" (D&C 63:25).

> with the New Jerusalem, so with the Jerusalem of old. Those assigned will build up the city.[13]

To reiterate the timing, Elder McConkie observed: "When that is to be remains to be seen, but that it will surely come to pass, as part of the preparation of the Lord's people for his glorious return, is as certain as that the sun shines or that the Great God is Lord of all."[14]

With nearly two hundred years of growth, experience, gathering of strength, and resources, both spiritually and temporally, Latter-day Saints ought to at least acknowledge the Lord is at the helm. He is more than good on His word. We just need to be better at "hearkening" unto His word. In the Doctrine and Covenants we read, "There is even now already in store sufficient, yea, even an abundance to redeem Zion, and establish her waste places, no more to be thrown down, were the churches, who call themselves after my name, willing to hearken to my voice."[15] The Lord also told the churches, "Let all these things be done in their time, but not in haste; and observe to have all things prepared before you."[16]

There is a wonderful preparation period taking place. "The Lord is at work with us."[17] He is gathering those throughout the world who want to contribute and be part. By helping ourselves and others receive the ordinances and covenants associated with the House of the Lord,

---

13. Bruce R. McConkie, *The Millennial Messiah*, 294. A few years later he would write: "After many days, a designated period in which we still live, those who are called, chosen, selected, appointed, and sent forth by the voice of the Spirit, as it speaks to the President of the Church, shall build the New Jerusalem and the holy temple to which the Lord Jesus Christ shall come in power and glory as the great Millennium is ushered in. In the meantime, our work as a people is to keep the commandments and sanctify ourselves so that if the call comes in our day, we shall be worthy to respond" (*A New Witness for the Articles of Faith*, 619).
14. Ibid., 281.
15. D&C 101:75.
16. D&C 101:72.
17. See Official Declaration 1, *Excerpts From the Three Addresses by President Wilford Woodruff Regarding the Manifesto*, second to the last paragraph.

we are taught how to qualify as a contributor to the establishment of Zion. In that temple experience we learn that our loyalty and consecration to The Church of Jesus Christ of Latter-day Saints and the building up of the Kingdom of God are crucial to the establishment of Zion. In temple worship, the Lord emphasizes the buildup to Zion.

We ought to enjoy and participate in the glorious buildup to the city of New Jerusalem. Spending a little more time with the "what" and "why" will help us be a little more at peace with the "where," "how," and "when." The building of a Zion city that will welcome a returning Zion city is very significant doctrine and a very significant event. "An Holy City" that will be built in majesty and glory.[18] As we continue to witness the telestial condition of the world, we will more anxiously desire to witness a return to beauty and order. The city of Zion will be the embodiment of "perfection of beauty."[19] Not only will it resonate with perfection and beauty, but it will also be the "joy of the whole earth."[20]

It will be a marvelous and yet brutal contrast to the troubled, unclean, and lawless cities of our day. So many cities are corrupt and collapsing. We ought to consider these things and our place as Latter-day Saints to stay off corruption and filth and seek for the perfection of beauty in our current situation and places of habitation.

---

18. Moses 7:62–64.
19. Psalm 50:2.
20. Psalm 48:2.

4

The Land of Zion and the New Jerusalem in the Doctrine and Covenants

"The command and the desire to establish Zion were present at the very beginning of this final great dispensation."[1]

The Doctrine and Covenants provides us an opportunity to understand the New Jerusalem and not be in complete ignorance. "Truths regarding the New Jerusalem have been revealed line upon line through Joseph Smith."[2] Imagine we have an image of the New Jerusalem that has been made into a puzzle. The pieces represent these "line upon line" revelations. The following contents of this chapter are intended to help you open the puzzle box and dump it out on a table. It is to give you some help turning the pieces right side up and placing them in their general location according to the image.

1. Richard Neitzel Holzapfel, "Establishing Zion in Preparation for the Second Coming," 108. In *Watch and Be Ready: Preparing for the Second Coming of the Lord*, Robert L. Millet, editor. 1994.
2. Donald W. Parry and Jay A Parry, *Understanding the Signs of the Times*, 1999. 155.

In chapters 2 and 3, I set forth some general thoughts on the *where*, *how*, and *when* of the New Jerusalem. To help us better understand *what* and *why*, I present the following references in the Doctrine and Covenants that deal directly with Zion and the New Jerusalem. Overall, there are 191 references to Zion in the Doctrine and Covenants. Not all those are references to Zion, the Holy City, the New Jerusalem. Nevertheless, the following references substantiate its significance in modern revelation. When studied in context of the complete revelation and the historical background, we begin to obtain a broader understanding of the Lord's purposes and will.

I will also note that 151 references to Zion are found in the Old Testament. Again, not all refer to the Latter-day Zion upon the American continent. It wasn't just prophets, priests, and kings who looked forward with joyful anticipation of Zion. I would also include the righteous patriarchs as ones who sought the delight and joy that would unfold in the last days. In the Book of Mormon, we have 42 references to Zion, with about two-thirds of those referring to Zion, the New Jerusalem. When Jesus Christ visited the Nephites, He spoke to them of the future city. A few references to Zion, the New Jerusalem, can be found in the New Testament (the spelling is Sion).

Joseph Fielding Smith understood the importance of what the Lord graciously extended to us concerning the New Jerusalem. He said: "Without modern revelation we would be in complete ignorance, as is the outside religious world, concerning the New Jerusalem. . . . These terms, Zion and Jerusalem, are used frequently interchangeably and if the Lord had not given us light we would have been as badly confused as are other people. However, there are many references which point clearly to the fact that Zion and Jerusalem are two separate and distinct places."[3]

Aware of potential ignorance, Moroni (and Ether) made clear: "Behold, Ether saw the days of Christ, and he spake concerning

---

3. *Church History and Modern Revelation*, vol. 2. See pages 171–172.

a New Jerusalem upon this land. And he spake also concerning the house of Israel, and the Jerusalem from whence Lehi should come—after it should be destroyed it should be built up again, a holy city unto the Lord; wherefore, it could not be a new Jerusalem for it had been in a time of old; but it should be built up again, and become a holy city of the Lord; and it should be built unto the house of Israel—And that a New Jerusalem should be built up upon this land, unto the remnant of the seed of Joseph, for which things there has been a type."[4]

Let's begin to connect some puzzle pieces.

I do not claim this as a conclusive list or a perfect list of verses from the Doctrine and Covenants. Looking at the verses as they unfolded sequentially in the Restoration allows us to comprehend themes, principles, and doctrines concerning Zion, the New Jerusalem. The following extraction of verses is a synopsis. (The dates designated in the reference column are the dates of the revelation). Additional chapters in this book will further investigate the themes, principles, and doctrines found in this overview. Let's see if we can put some of this puzzle together. Take time to dump the puzzle on the table and spread out the pieces. Read the following content and see if you can connect a few pieces to help bring the image into focus. What themes, ideas, principles, and doctrines concerning Zion, the New Jerusalem, come to you?

D&C Reference	Synopsis
D&C 28:9 (September 1830)	Geography/location of the city of Zion to be revealed according to the Lord's directive.
D&C 29:7–8 (September 26, 1830)	There is a center gathering place on the American continent to prepare the Lord's elect for desolations that are coming.

4. Ether 13:4–6.

D&C 35:24 (December 1830)	If we keep the commandments and our covenants, Zion will "rejoice upon the hills and flourish." Often in the revelations Zion is spoken as a *cause* and a *place*. This reference could allude to both.
D&C 38:17–22 (January 2, 1831)	The Lord refers to Zion as a "land of promise, a land flowing with milk and honey, upon which there shall be no curse when the Lord cometh." Zion is to be a land of inheritance for the faithful in the Millennium and when the earth is celestialized. Jesus Christ will be king and lawgiver. We will have no laws, but His laws, when He comes.
D&C 42:8–9 (February 9, 1831)	Westward migration and the building up of the Lord's Church will proceed until the Lord designates the New Jerusalem to be prepared and His people gathered.
D&C 42:35, 62, 67 (February 9, 1831)	By consecration, Saints are to provide resources and additional property to be used to purchase lands for the New Jerusalem. First reference to purchasing in the Doctrine and Covenants. The Lord assured the Saints that if He is petitioned, He would reveal the location of New Jerusalem. Church covenants would be given to sustain Zion.
D&C 45:65-73 (March 7, 1831)	Another reference to "purchase" the land. Location again stated as forthcoming. The Lord gives several details, descriptions, and promises concerning Zion. These verses should be studied closely.

D&C 48:4–6 (March 10, 1831)	Saints told to "save all the money that [they] can" so that eventually they can "purchase land for an inheritance, even the city." These early Saints would "make a commencement to lay the foundation of the city." First reference to the gathering to the city by families.
D&C 49:25 (May 7, 1831)	First reference to Zion as an "appointed" place. Also, first reference to being "assembled." Usually, the language is "gathered." Either way it represents a collective body. "Assembled" may emphasize that people have been brought together or fit together from different parts.
D&C 52:2–5, 42–43 (June 6, 1831)	The Lord said, "I will consecrate" the land of Missouri for those who are "heirs according to the covenant." This is the first reference to Missouri in the Doctrine and Covenants. Joseph and Sidney are told to go there as soon as possible and learn of the place of inheritance. The Lord warns them that the land is currently the land of their enemies. The Lord will "hasten the city in its time."
D&C 57:1–5, 14–15 (July 20, 1831)	Land of Missouri designated as a place for the gathering of the Saints. The Lord reiterates the city of Zion will be built here, even identifying the center place, Independence, and a spot for a temple. Another reference to purchasing the land round about. Second reference to "families" being sent to establish the area under the direction of the bishop.

D&C 58:6–7, 17, 49–53 (August 1, 1831)	Joseph and others "honored in laying the foundation" for the "Zion of God." A bishop (agent) is designated to receive moneys "to purchase lands in Zion." Sidney Rigdon appointed to write a description of Zion, as well as the Lord's will concerning its establishment. The Lord desires them to purchase the "whole region of country, as soon as time will permit."
D&C 58:54–57 (August 1, 1831)	Workmen for the development of Zion will be sent by the bishop and agent of the Church. Presiding elders of the Church will receive revelation from time to time concerning the work of gathering. The buildup of the city of Zion will be done in order.
D&C 62:2–6 (August 13, 1831)	This revelation is in context of initial missionaries coming and going from the land of Zion. They were told to assemble upon Zion "and rejoice together, and offer a sacrament unto the Most High." Also, the Lord confirms that "the faithful among you should be preserved and rejoice together in the land of Missouri. *I, the Lord, promise the faithful and cannot lie."*
D&C 63:24–37, 40–41 (August 30, 1831)	The Lord again states the Saints should assemble upon the land of Zion in order. They are to purchase lands lawfully and avoid bloodshed as their enemies are stirred by Satan. He warns those who will be gathered that they will be "scourged from city to city." The land of Zion shall be a refuge from the desolations. Joseph Smith given discernment on who is to go to the land of Zion.

D&C 64:33–36, 38, 41 (September 11, 1831)	The willing hearts and minds receive an inheritance in Zion. The rebellious are cut off. "Inhabitants of Zion shall judge all things pertaining to Zion." In her sovereignty she "shall flourish" and God's glory will be upon her.
D&C 133:2–5, 9, 21–25, 32, 56 (November 3, 1831)	We are to prepare and sanctify ourselves to gather upon the Land of Zion. We are to flee Babylon. Jesus Christ will "utter his voice out of Zion." At a designated time, the Lord will turn the land of Zion (and the land of Jerusalem) back into their own place, and "the earth shall be like as it was in the days before it was divided." Resurrected Saints will stand on the right of Jesus Christ at "Mount Zion and upon the holy city, the New Jerusalem."
D&C 68:25–31 (November 1831)	Inhabitants of Zion are to teach their children to understand the principles and ordinances of the gospel. This includes prayer and observing the Sabbath. The Lord rebukes idleness and greed and will not have either of them in Zion.
D&C 69:1–6 (November 11, 1831)	Someone faithful and true to take "moneys" to the land of Zion. Zion is a "seat and a place" for "writing and making a history" as well as receiving the accounts of elders' labors throughout the earth. Emphasis seems to be on record keeping "for the good" of "rising generations" that shall live in Zion.

D&C 72:9–19, 24–26 (December 4, 1831)	"Every man (family) that cometh up to Zion must lay all things before the bishop in Zion." Anyone appointed by the holy spirit" (see D&C 63:41) to "go up to Zion" must carry a "certificate" (endorsement) from presiding elders or bishop where they were residing.
D&C 82:14–20 (April 26, 1832)	Zion must "increase in beauty and holiness" and put on "her beautiful garments." The stakes of Zion "must be strengthened." First reference in the D&C to *stakes of* Zion. Inhabitants of Zion will covenant to consecrate and seek the interest of one another and make sure all needs, and righteous wants are met. This is to be an "everlasting order" for them and future leaders and Saints.
D&C 84:1–4, 31–32 (September 22-23, 1832)	Specific declaration reinforcing the Saints to be gathered "upon Mount Zion, which shall be the city of New Jerusalem" ("The city of the living God." See D&C 76:66 also for reference to New Jerusalem as Mount Zion.) The temple to built will be the cornerstone of the city to be built. The city to be built "by the gathering of the Saints." The people will be "filled with the glory of the Lord" in the "Lord's house."
D&C 84:96–102 (September 22–23, 1832)	As the Lord subdues unrighteousness and sweeps wickedness from the earth, knowledge of the Lord will sweep the earth. A new song will be sung by the inhabitants of the earth emphasizing that Zion from above and Zion from beneath shall assimilate and truth be established.

D&C 90:36–37 (March 8, 1833)	The Lord states He will labor and plead with Zion. He will "chasten her until she overcomes and is clean." He confirms that "Zion will not be moved out of her place."
D&C 97:3, 10–28 (August 2, 1833)	A school to be established in Zion (school of the prophets). By tithing and for the salvation of Zion, a temple should be built to the pattern which the Lord had previously shown. Nations of the earth will honor Zion and she will escape desolations if she does what the Lord requires. The Lord will multiply blessings upon her.
D&C 100:13 (October 12, 1833)	Zion will be redeemed, "although she is chastened for a little season." This revelation was received after the brutal experiences of expulsion the Saints had experienced in Jackson County.
D&C 101:16–23 (December 16-17, 1833)	The Lord tells the Saints to be comforted and reminds them "there is none other place appointed concerning the city of Zion. All the blessings and promises concern Zion shall be fulfilled. Though temporarily scattered and deferred in building the city, the Saints will return and "build up the waste places of Zion." He also references stakes of Zion as other places for gathering.

D&C 101:42–63, 68–75 (December 16-17, 1833)	The Lord gives the parable "concerning the redemption of Zion." He promises that "by and by" [He] will come with the residue of [His] house and possess the land." There is a preparation period. He tells them to continue to buy land in the region of Jackson County, "and the counties round about." We are to hearken unto His voice.
D&C 103:15–20 (February 24, 1834)	Jesus Christ will raise up unto His people a man like unto Moses. A comparison to the Lord leading Moses and the children of Israel out of Egypt is made. They were "led out of bondage by power." So will the redemption of Zion come by power. "In time [we] shall possess the goodly land."
D&C 105 (June 22, 1834)	The entirety of this section should be carefully studied not only in historical context but also with the future of Zion, the New Jerusalem in mind. Perhaps one line in this section suffices here. "Zion cannot be built unless it is by the principles of the law of the celestial kingdom, otherwise I cannot receive her unto myself."
D&C 109:39 (March 27, 1836)	The righteous out of other cities are to be sought for and are to come forth to Zion and/or one of her stakes.
D&C 113:7–8 (March 1838)	Zion will return to power when those called to bring it forth "put on the authority of the priesthood."
D&C 115:5–6 (April 26, 1838)	Gathering upon the Land of Zion and her stakes will provide a defense and refuge.

D&C 119:1–7 (July 8, 1838)	Surplus property is to be consecrated. Tithing is a standing law for those who gather upon the land of Zion. As all obey the law they will "sanctify the land of Zion unto the [Lord]." It will become "most holy."
D&C 124:6, 49–51 (January 19, 1841)	The Lord will call upon "kings and authorities . . . to give heed to the light and glory of Zion." The Lord accepted the offering of those foundational Saints who did their best to build a city and a temple in Missouri. He will visit the head of those who hinder His work.
D&C 136:18, 31 (January 1847)	As the Saints were pushing westward the Lord reminded them that Zion would "be redeemed in [His] own due time." The Saints are to be "tried in all things" to be prepared for the glory of Zion.

Before the fulfillment of all these particulars concerning Zion, the New Jerusalem, the work of gathering will continue to push on. As people accept the ordinances and the covenants of the House of the Lord, the Lord will place in their hearts the cause of Zion. Joseph Smith, Oliver Cowdery, Hyrum Smith, and Joseph Knight Sr. were all told to "keep the commandments, and seek to bring forth and establish the cause of Zion."[5] I believe this is our charge as well. Our vision and efforts to "bring forth and establish the cause of Zion" are multiplied by being taught and inspired through temple worship.

For emphasis, contemplate the following verses not in the synopsis above. "Keep all the commandments and covenants by which ye are

5. D&C 6:6; 11:6; 12:6.

bound; and I will cause the heavens to shake for your good, and Satan shall tremble and Zion shall rejoice upon the hills and flourish; And Israel shall be saved in mine own due time; and by the keys which I have given shall they be led, and no more be confounded at all."[6] Isaiah saw likewise. "[The Lord] shall cause them that come of Jacob to take root: Israel shall blossom and bud, and fill the face of the world with fruit."[7] This has to happen first. It's in the process of happening now.

As we consider the teachings from the Doctrine and Covenants, we see the Lord's order and timing unfolding. We see His wisdom and His blessings being poured out. What He told Latter-day Saints in the first generation of this dispensation wasn't fanciful or exaggerated teachings regarding a holy city. There is a glorious, yet quiet crescendo happening. We can't expect immediacy. The Lord will help us. "For Zion's sake [He] will not hold [His] peace. . . . Salvation will come to people who will have Him to be their God. Such people will be known as "The holy people," who will be "Sought out, A city not forsaken."[8]

Therefore, we need to learn and acquire godly attributes. Of which President Lorenzo Snow taught:

> Purity, virtue, fidelity, and godliness must be sought for ambitiously, or the crown cannot be worn. Those principles must be incorporated with ourselves—woven into our constitutions—become part of us, making us a centre, a fountain of truth, of equity, justice, and mercy, of all that is good and great: that from us may proceed light, the life, the power, and the law to direct, to govern and assist to save a wondering world. . . . These qualifications can be had only as they are sought and obtained. . . . Godliness cannot be conferred, but must be acquired—a fact of which the religious world seem strangely and lamentably unconscious.[9]

---

6. D&C 35:24–25.
7. Isaiah 27:6.
8. Isaiah 62:1, 11–12.
9. *Biography and Family Record of Lorenzo Snow*, 193.

While relying on the Lord's great blessings and power, Enoch and Melchizedek had to labor with their people for years to obtain a Zion state of existence. Their acquisition of godly attributes didn't come instantaneously. They were not a Zion people all at once, in the snap of a finger. Or dare I say, at the instant of several divine revelations being received by them (or in our dispensation, by Joseph Smith). Enoch and Melchizedek had to teach the commandments and preach repentance for years.[10] Enoch had to continue his preaching in righteousness and then start to build a city. As this was occurring the Lord showed Enoch that "Zion, *in the process of time*, was taken up into heaven."[11] Melchizedek's experience many years later followed the same pattern.

We are following the same pattern. It is a glorious, quiet crescendo. The revelations above in the Doctrine and Covenants are only a few verses that confirm this pattern, this crescendo. If we are growing impatient in the Lord's "process of time," we might want to consider to what extent we are receiving the preaching of righteousness and heeding its call to acquire godly attributes. Both the Father and His Son have great interest in our process of acquisition. They are extending Their help and power to those who choose Their way. The building of a holy city can't happen without a people who choose to walk with our Heavenly Father and His Son Jesus Christ.

> "A fact of which the religious world seems strangely and lamentably unconscious."[12]

---

10. Alma 13:6, 18. This is a marvelous chapter to consider concerning how to establish a Zion people and how to seek the welfare of Zion yourself.
11. Moses 7:18–21.
12. *Biography and Family Record of Lorenzo Snow*, 193.

5

Imminent Desolation

"We must acknowledge that the building up of Zion occurs in tumultuous times."[1]

Unruly water. Unwelcome fire. Calamitous winds. Instant earthquakes. Eruptions of the earth. Severe lightning and thunder. Destructive hailstorms. Troubling famines and pestilences. Why?[2]

Many of you have experienced some of these. Perhaps you have witnessed some of them face to face or from a close peripheral. Imminent desolation may not be the most enjoyable subject to read and think about. We are talking destruction, disruption, and death. It may be wise to remember up front that the "Lord God worketh not in darkness. He doeth not anything save it be for the benefit of the world; for he loveth the world."[3]

1. Elder D. Todd Christofferson "Preparing for the Lord's Return," *Ensign*, May 2020.
2. D&C 43:25.
3. 2 Nephi 26:23–24.

I believe desolation needs consideration as we place Zion, the New Jerusalem, in context. I will set forth four types of desolation in this chapter.

To make sure some readers will not accuse me of being in the top row of the bleachers or just a gloomy pickle sucker quarantined in my house, I quote the Lord's words on this subject. To the Nephites who survived the destruction that *He caused* (see 3 Nephi 9), we learn what will happen in the last days as the building up of Zion begins to occur. To the Nephites He was speaking, this would have been all too familiar. They just went through it themselves when they heard Him say:

> Yea, wo be unto the Gentiles except they repent; for it shall come to pass in that day, saith the Father, that I will cut off thy horses out of the midst of thee, and I will destroy thy chariots; And I will cut off the cities of thy land, and throw down all thy strongholds; And I will cut off witchcrafts out of thy land, and thou shalt have no more soothsayers; Thy graven images I will also cut off, and thy standing images out of the midst of thee, and thou shalt no more worship the works of thy hands; And I will pluck up thy groves out of the midst of thee; so will I destroy thy cities.
>
> And it shall come to pass that all lyings, and deceivings, and envyings, and strifes, and priestcrafts, and whoredoms, shall be done away. For it shall come to pass, saith the Father, that at that day whosoever will not repent and come unto my Beloved Son, them will I cut off from among my people, O house of Israel; And I will execute vengeance and fury upon them, even as upon the heathen, such as they have not heard.[4]

Jesus Christ is telling us that cities will be destroyed. Transportation and the safety and security of these cities will be brought to nothing. The gross wickedness in them will be done away. Read the references in this footnote for understanding of the Lord's declared

4. 3 Nephi 21:14–21. I would also consider 1 Nephi 21:8.

desolations.[5] He had much more to say on the subject.

Those of us floating in the cares and pleasure of the world may not be able to discern real dangers before us. The dangers of ignoring and denying what the Savior warned He would bring upon us if we do not repent. We were once reminded by devoted disciple and apostle Neal A. Maxwell: "Noah and those with him had to let go of their world or perish with it."[6] We ought to talk about and know what is coming. It heightens our spiritual and temporal preparation individually and collectively.

> "The great and wise of ancient days have failed in all their attempts to promote eternal power, peace, and happiness. Their nations have crumbled to pieces; their thrones have been cast down in their turn; and their cities, and their mightiest works of art have been annihilated; or their dilapidated towers, or time worn monuments have left us but feeble traits of their former magnificence, and ancient grandeur. They proclaim as with a voice of thunder, those imperishable truths—that man's strength is weakness, his wisdom is folly, his glory is his shame?"
>
> —Joseph Smith
>
> (Joseph Smith, Editorial, "The Government of God," Nauvoo, Hancock Co., IL, 15 July 1842; in *Times and Seasons*, 15 July 1842, 3:855–858.)

According to the Savior's instruction to the Nephites in 3 Nephi 21, desolation will come prior to the city of New Jerusalem being started.

---

5. D&C 29:9–27; D&C 45:16–45; D&C 88:87–92; Matthew 24; Joseph Smith—Matthew 24 (which adds about 450 words to Matthew in the Bible. It also should be noted, "The text in Matthew 24 in the King James Version has many unclear passages and its organization is confusing. The Prophet Joseph Smith's work makes both the historical chronology of this prophecy and the doctrinal significance of its teachings plain and inspiring" (*The Pearl of Great Price Student Manual*, 43). These two comparable chapters refer to the "abomination of desolation."
6. See Elder Neal A. Maxwell, *Wherefore, Ye Must Press Forward* (Salt Lake City: Deseret Book, 1977), 13.

Some may say, "Ryan, the Lord told us to 'talk not about judgments.'"[7] In June of 1834 the Lord cautioned members of Zion's Camp and members of the Church living in Clay County, Missouri, and adjoining counties to not talk about judgments. It helps to understand the context of the situation at that time in Missouri. I will let the reader discover that context on their own.[8]

But the truth of the matter is, in other revelations the Lord does give us a charge to speak of and warn of the desolations coming. It is one thing for me to pronounce a judgment upon a person or people in my pride, and quite another to warn of desolation (especially the ones He sets forth). Remember, during his second appearance to Joseph Smith in the early morning hours of September 22, 1823, Moroni "informed [Joseph Smith] of great judgments which were coming upon the earth, with great desolations." He, Moroni, was sent to talk about them.[9]

A glimpse of that charge to warn of such desolations would come a few years later: "Every man should take righteousness in his hands and faithfulness upon his loins, and lift a warning voice unto the inhabitants of the earth; and declare both by word and by flight that desolation shall come upon the wicked."[10] Another one states: "Go ye forth as your circumstances shall permit, in your several callings, unto the great and notable cities and villages, reproving the world in righteousness of all their unrighteous and ungodly deeds, setting forth clearly and understandingly the desolation of abomination in the last days."[11]

Situations and circumstances in which we have not heard of are before us. We ought to think about and know a thing or two about desolation. It's coming. In many instances it is happening right under our noses.

---

7. D&C 105:24.
8. Refer to *Revelations in Context*, 213–217. Obtainable at ChurchofJesusChrist.org.
9. See Joseph Smith—History 1:45.
10. D&C 63:37.
11. D&C 84:117. There are plenty more examples.

In speaking to Enoch, founder of the Zion that was translated, the Lord said: "And the day shall come that the earth shall rest, *but* before that day the heavens shall be darkened, and a veil of darkness shall cover the earth; and the heavens shall shake, and also the earth; and great tribulations shall be among the children of men, *but* my people will I preserve."[12] I recommend you consider the conjunction word "but" in this verse. It sets a part two distinct thoughts.

Speaking to another generation of Saints, the Lord said "that the gathering upon the land of Zion, and upon her stakes, may be for a defense and for a refuge from the storm, and from wrath when it shall be poured out without mixture upon the whole earth."[13] And in similar language He would reiterate: "Wherefore the decree hath gone forth from the Father that they shall be gathered in unto one place upon the face of this land, to prepared their hearts and be prepared in all things against the day when tribulation and desolation are sent forth upon the wicked."[14]

Before addressing such desolations by the hand of Lord, let's consider a few other types of desolation. Each one is evident and occurring, even as you read.

Individual Desolation. This is best summed up with the following: "How are they brought into desolation, as in a moment! They are utterly consumed with terrors."[15] Fear or terrors can paralyze us individually and collectively. What causes these terrors? To name a few, lawlessness, oppressive governments or violent factions of society, sicknesses, perversions, economic strains, depleted resources from failing community infrastructure that forces change in lifestyle and places of residence, and of course, Mother Nature's force. But simply, our own disobedient lives leave us desolate. Continuing in a sinful life leaves us fearful.

---

12. Moses 7:61. See also 2 Nephi 8:16.
13. D&C 115:6.
14. D&C 29:8.
15. Psalm 73:19.

In fear, we inhibit or are void of the spirit of the Lord. We walk in the pride of our own hearts and the blindness of our own eyes. Isaiah left the imagery of a fallen people separated from their God in this language: "Their feet run to evil, and they make haste to shed innocent blood: their thoughts are thoughts of iniquity; wasting and destruction are in their paths. . . . [They] grope for the wall like the blind, and [they] grope as if [they] had no eyes: [they] stumble at noonday as in the night; [they] are in desolate places as dead men."[16]

Speaking of dead men, the Savior used this metaphor to describe those desolate individuals in His day: "Woe unto you, scribes and Pharisees, hypocrites! For ye are like unto whited sepulchres, which indeed appear beautiful outward, but are within full of dead men's bones, and of all uncleanness."[17] Rarely is an unsettled and disobedient life addressed or confronted in public. "The fruits of rebellion [are] indeed . . . desolation."[18]

Individual desolation is a very real thing. We don't have to look far. In most cases inner reflection brings us to the first casualty. Far too many people are personally ruined. Multiplied bad decisions and habits have left so many desolate. This personal desolation is a catalyst to family ruin and community ruin. This desolation causes an inner fear that will never subside without the help of Jesus Christ.

Demographic Desolation. Children move on. Families sell the farm and leave homesteads. Bigger opportunities are found elsewhere. Pick your region. For me, nowhere is this so obvious than in the Midwest (USA). Several small towns dot the landscape. Many of these towns are in bad shape. Not only have their children moved on, but so have their grandfather's industries. Major highways and new railways have bypassed them. With reasons related to my employment I have been in many of these towns in Missouri, Illinois, and Iowa. I have also seen the evidence of demographic desolation in Pennsylvania, Ohio, New York, and Texas.

---

16. Isaiah 59:7, 10.
17. Matthew 23:27.
18. "O, America, America." *Ensign*, Nov. 1979.

Any state in the union has demographic desolation. Towns are falling apart. Segments, and in many instances large portions of cities, feel like and look like something from an eerie movie. Some may rebound and revitalize as world events ebb and flow. But many will not. Such a state breeds trouble in so many other ways. Those who can, choose another place of residence.

Citizen Inflicted Desolation. It is before our eyes. The evidence is piling up. People are deserting cities once considered glamorous. Once considered a safe and healthy place to live and vacation, now they are unclean, unsafe, and dilapidated. Even before the 2020 protesting, riots, and looting, many American cities were already crumbling and declining in population. Segments of major cities were already desolate. Such cities are now dealing with occupancy desolation in business office spaces and apartment and condominium rentals. With new work opportunities remotely, this may never be the same.

As I write, Chicago civic leaders are pleading for food stores to remain in the south side of their city. But Chicago should know very well what has happened to their region neighbors Cleveland, Detroit, and St. Louis over the years. Unchecked murder, assaults, and a host of other atrocities have people desperately trying to go elsewhere. These are not isolated to the Midwest. It's happening everywhere. In late 2020, an alarming number of police officers left the force in Portland, Oregon. Why? Because of citizen-inflicted desolation.[19]

The citizen-inflicted desolation enflamed by rogue individuals and organized groups in all parts of the land bring us face to face with the imagery Isaiah had to convey to backsliding Judah, "the breach ready to fall, swelling out in a high wall, whose breaking

19. Elder Holland reiterated that a prevailing message of the Book of Mormon and its authors "prophetically warn us that violence and conflict will be a signature characteristic of relationships in the last days" ("Not as the World Giveth," April 2021 general conference).

cometh suddenly at an instant."[20] Some cities are in trouble. They are imploding. Again, this is not an enjoyable observation, but it is true. We must not try to turn a blind eye.

The wicked will destroy the wicked,[21] but they also cause a lot of alarming injustices for honest, law-abiding people who want a peaceful existence. Wicked characters and their continual behaviors cause a lot a heartache and a lot of unnecessary interruptions. They even take the lives of the innocent and righteous.[22] But the Lord will righteously sort these out and "take even them who he will take, and preserveth in life them whom he will preserve."[23] He will extend power to His covenant people. He will provide for their safety.[24] This should be expected and quite noticeably in the coming days.

In explaining some of Isaiah's teachings to his brothers, Nephi recorded, "For the time soon cometh that the fulness of the wrath of God shall be poured out upon all the children of men; for he will not suffer that the wicked shall destroy the righteous. Wherefore, he will preserve the righteous by his power, even if it so be that the fulness of his wrath must come, and the righteous be preserved, even unto the destruction of their enemies by fire. Wherefore, the righteous need not fear; for thus saith the prophet, they shall be saved, even if it so be as by fire."[25]

The Lord's Declared Desolations. The previous scriptural citation brings us to the fourth type of desolation: the judgments of the Lord. Years ago, President N. Eldon Tanner taught: "It is hard to understand why so many people are prepared to accept facts as recorded by historians in secular history and yet refuse to accept

---

20. Isaiah 30:13.
21. Mormon 4:5 and D&C 63:32–33.
22. Consider as an example the women the children who believed the words of Alma and Amulek and were destroyed by fire by the ruling and disobedient class of Ammonihah.
23. D&C 63:3.
24. 1 Nephi 14:14.
25. 1 Nephi 22:16–17. See also 1 Nephi 14:12–14; 2 Nephi 6:13–15.

ecclesiastical history as recorded in the scriptures by men whose characters are beyond reproach, and even refuse to believe, as having come from the Lord, prophecies that have been fulfilled and verified by secular history."[26]

Ecclesiastical history has plenty to say on the subject. Where are the bright lights of Babylon and the towering high rises of Sodom and Gomorrah? Where are the markets of many Mayan cities? Why are some ancient cities now under water? Nineveh is no longer. Many ancient cities in the empires of Assyria and Rome had abrupt endings.

Elder Mark E. Petersen posed some questions: "And what is the lesson in all of this? It is that no people can fight God and live! Every nation will feel a chastening hand if it turns its back upon the Ruler of Heaven and violates his eternal precepts. . . . Does our modern world accept or reject Jesus Christ? And if we reject him, does the prospect of desolation concern us? . . . Does our modern world risk the same kind of desolation that came upon the ancient world—and for the same reason?"[27]

These are not comfortable questions to confront. But they must be confronted. "We must acknowledge," Elder D. Todd Christofferson suggests, "that the building up of Zion occurs in tumultuous times—'a day of wrath, a day of burning, a day of desolation, of weeping, of mourning, and of lamentation; and as a whirlwind it shall come upon all the face of the earth, saith the Lord.'"[28]

Trusting in and serving Jesus Christ is the answer. That trust in Jesus Christ is going to need to be deep and genuine as many, perhaps all, feel the sting and the immediacy of disruptions and desolations. We will need to be remarkably calm and spiritually resilient in difficult circumstances. The inhabitants in the world will observe how people who trust in Jesus Christ respond. Our fortitude may

---

26. "Warnings from Outer Space," October 1972 general conference. Interesting title for his address.
27. "O, America, America." *Ensign*, Nov. 1979.
28. "Preparing for the Lord's Return," *Ensign*, May 2019.

even influence some to leave sin and false traditions behind and join the covenant path.

Joseph Smith counseled what we can do to prepare for these disruptions as we move toward the buildup of Zion: "We know not what we shall be called to pass through before Zion is delivered and established; therefore, we have a great need to live near to God, and always to be in strict obedience to all his commandments, that we may have a conscience void of offense toward God and man."[29] The Savior (in Luke's account of His stated desolations) urged all to "watch ye therefore, and pray always, *that ye may be accounted worthy to escape all these things that shall come to pass*, and to stand before the Son of man."[30]

---

29. *Teachings of Presidents of the Church: Joseph Smith*, 233.
30. Luke 21:36; italics for emphasis.

6

Geography and Topography of the New Jerusalem

"As far as the eye can reach the beautiful rolling prairies lay spread out like a sea of meadows."[1]

At its equator, the earth is spinning at 1,000 miles per hour. This consistent rotation has been occurring for a very long time. Couple this rotation with the earth's orbit around the sun, which is up to 67,000 miles per hour. Our solar system orbits the center of the Milky Way Galaxy at just under 500,000 miles per hour. Sit still and think about that for a minute. In that minute you will have traveled thousands of miles in a remarkable orchestrating way.[2] This may change as God's

1. "History, 1838–1856, volume A-1 [23 December 1805–30 August 1834]," The Joseph Smith Papers, 138, accessed December 17, 2020, https://www.josephsmithpapers.org/paper-summary/history-1838-1856-volume-a-1-23-december-1805-30-august-1834/144. Or, *History of the Church*, 1:197.
2. See Abraham 3:1–10. See also Andrew Fraknoi, "How Fast Are You Moving When You Are Sitting Still?" Online, *The Universe in the Classroom*. April 2007, No. 71.

purposes unfold. Let all the creations keep spinning, while you keep reading without getting dizzy.

Think for a moment about the brilliant places on earth you have visited and seen with your natural eyes. Consider the marvelous geography of your own local environment. When is the last time you found some appreciation in the topography of where you live? Where is one of the admiring places of the earth for you? Why? You don't have to go far in many instances. "Isn't it ironic," Elder Steven E. Snow quipped, "that we will often travel many miles to see the wonders of nature or the creations of man, but yet ignore the beauty in our own backyard?"[3]

This earth, without question, has variety and beauty. Nonetheless, like us, it, too, is in a fallen state. It will be redeemed by Heavenly Father and Jesus Christ. Because of a unique statement by the Lord about land masses, the concept of geography and topography should be visited. I began with some particulars about planets. Let's come back to earth. Everyone's "backyard" could experience bit of a change.

What did the geography of the earth look like in its paradisiacal form? What did it look like after the Fall in Adam and Eve's day? What did it look like after the Flood? Were there differences in the days of Peleg, in which the earth was divided? [4] Were there always enormous mountains and long valleys since the first days of creation? In three of our four creation accounts we learn that dry land appeared.[5] (As depicted in our temple geographic account of creation, we have the distinction of mountains and hills, and so on.) What will be the features when the earth is renewed and receives it paradisiacal glory?[6]

---

3. See "Gratitude," *Ensign*, Nov. 2001. I highly recommend you read the first few paragraphs of this address. He tells a great story that pounds his point. This is a worthwhile story that could be used in teaching.
4. Genesis 10:25.
5. See Genesis 1, Moses 2, and Abraham 4.
6. "Everything is to be brought back as nearly as it is possible to its position as it was in the beginning. The mountains, we are informed, are to be thrown down, the valleys are to be exalted, and 'the earth shall be like as it was in the days before it was divided'" (Joseph Fielding Smith, *The Restoration of All Things*, 294–95).

The earth will return to its pristine abode as it was at creation. It will be restored. Joseph Fielding Smith taught, "This earth is to be renewed and brought back to the condition in which it was before it was cursed through the fall of Adam."[7] It now is in a telestial condition. When it is renewed it will be in a terrestrial condition. Ultimately, the earth will become a celestial sphere.[8] So, expect, plan, and be ready for some adjustments. Regardless of the changes, the grandeur and beauty of the earth will only become more astonishing.

When the surviving Nephites and Lamanites experienced what they did at the death and resurrection of Jesus Christ, we are told they gathered after the destruction and "were marveling and wondering one with another, and were showing one to another the great and marvelous change which had taken place."[9] Recall some cities were buried up in the earth, some in the depths of the sea or other large bodies of water. The land was trembling, rending, groaning, and described as accompanied by tumultuous noises.[10] These were noises of a great storm, tempests, and thunder that shook the earth, accompanied with sharp lightnings, fire, quaking, and whirlwinds.[11]

This left the land very different than a few days before. "The face of the whole earth became deformed. . . . The rocks were rent in twain; they were broken up upon the face of the whole earth . . . broken fragments, and in seams and in cracks, upon all the face of the land."[12] Of course this was fulfillment of Samuel the Lamanite's accurate description of what would happen to their land when the Savior would "yield up the ghost."[13]

---

7. Joseph Fielding Smith, *Doctrines of Salvation*, 1:85.
8. D&C 88:17–21.
9. 3 Nephi 11:1.
10. See 3 Nephi 10:9, 13.
11. See 3 Nephi 8:5–14.
12. 3 Nephi 8:16–19.
13. See Helaman 14:21–22.

Other scriptural accounts provide topographical occurrences and situations to consider.[14] But before I get to earth's topography in the last days, let's recall the situation of the earth at Adam's day. President Joseph Fielding Smith observed:

> We are committed to the fact that Adam dwelt on this American continent. But when Adam dwelt here, it was not the American continent, nor was it the Western Hemisphere, for all the land was in *one place*, and all the water was in one place. There was no Atlantic Ocean separating the hemispheres. "And God said, let the Waters under the heaven be gathered together unto *one place*, and let the dry land appear: and it was so. And God called the dry land Earth; and the gathering together of the waters called he Seas: and God saw that it was good." If all the water was in *one place*, then naturally all the land was in one place; therefore, the shape of the earth, as to the water and the land surface, was not as we find it today.[15]

The Lord will revisit the deformations of the earth that have occurred with the Fall and the subsequent events that have followed for over 6,000 years. The cataclysmic events that have altered the original creation will have to be addressed. If He (and others) created the earth in the first place, He not only can subdue it, but He can also restore it. There is a new heaven and a new earth on the horizon. It will be a "fulness" and a remarkable replenishment of God's creations.[16]

What does this all mean for the center place of Zion (the New Jerusalem) and the accompanying stakes of Zion? What can we expect as this restoration and move to a terrestrial state occurs?

---

14. A few examples: Genesis 10:25; Numbers 16:30–35; Moses 7:14, Ether 12:30. Earthquakes, volcanoes, underwater tumults, tsunamis, landslides, sink holes, and other forms of eruptions are naturally occurring events that can rapidly change Earth's surface. The Lord said He would use these to get the attention of the unrepentant (D&C 43:25).
15. *Doctrines of Salvation* 3:74.
16. D&C 29:23–25

Sometime at, or near the Second Coming of Jesus Christ, He will do the following:

> Utter his voice out of Zion, and he shall speak from Jerusalem, and his voice shall be heard among all people. And it shall be a voice as the voice of many waters, and as the voice of a great thunder, which shall break down the mountains, and the valleys shall not be found. He shall command the great deep, and it shall be driven back into the north countries, and the islands shall become one land; And the land of Jerusalem and the land of Zion shall be turned back into their own place, and the earth shall be like as it was in the days before it was divided. And the Lord, even the Savior, shall stand in the midst of his people, and shall reign over all flesh.[17]

This ought to change things. I suppose we can expect some magnificent changes in geography. There will be a day when people will be gathered "marveling and wondering" at changes that have occurred with the earth's appearance.[18] A prophecy by Ezekiel accords with this great change described in the Doctrine and Covenants verses you just read. He recorded that "mountains shall be thrown down, and the steep places shall fall."[19] Will some mountains be no more? Will some valleys disappear? They have done so in other ages and dispensations. Are we talking countless and continuous rolling hills being more predominant? I don't know. The earth's surface has grand extremes in topography, many of which are not inhabitable. They are beautiful in their own current state but not inhabitable. On the following page are some topographical maps of the United States today. They are fascinating to review as we ponder this topic.

---

17. D&C 133:21–25.
18. Again, 3 Nephi 11:1.
19. See all of Ezekiel 38:18–23. He records that all living creatures (fishes, fowls, beasts, insects and man) will be shaken and come to know Jesus Christ is Lord.

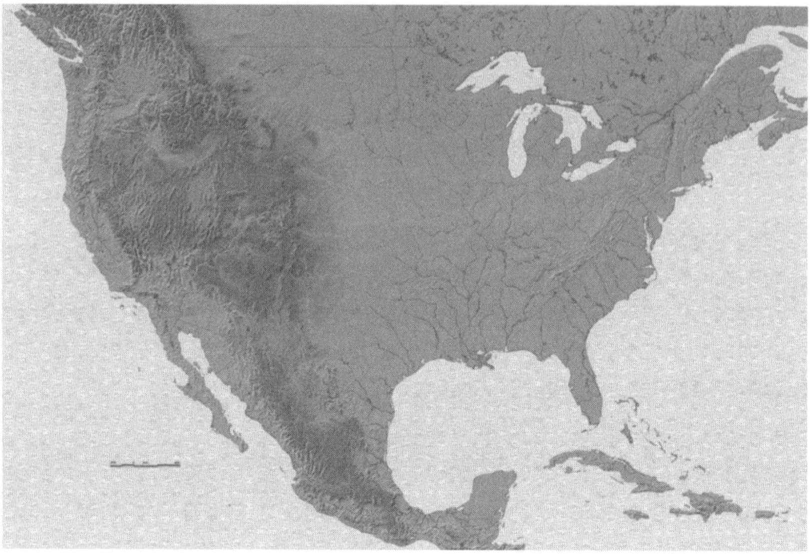

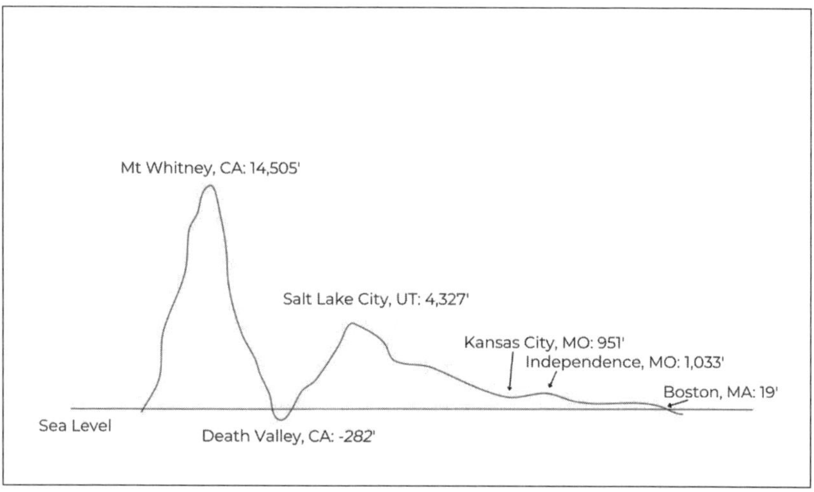

Image created by Joelle Humphries

I don't pretend to understand fully what it means that mountains will be broken down and valleys shalt not be found. Going back to the destruction at the time of the Nephites, we learn of a reversal of the mountains and valleys they were familiar with at that time. Samuel gave this description: "There shall be great tempests, and there shall be many mountains laid low, like unto a valley, and there shall be many places which are now called valleys which shall become mountains, whose height is great."[20] He drew attention to very high mountains. Perhaps heights they were not accustomed to viewing. We just don't know.

In the same revelation that talks about the mountains being broken down and valleys not being found, we also have reference to the "boundaries of the everlasting hills." The Savior and His appointed servants would stand within these boundaries of the everlasting hills and welcome the lost tribes of Israel to Zion.[21] There are hills, and then there are mountains. In our day we seem to distinguish them by these two distinct names. In scripture sometimes they could be used more synonymously than they are used today.

Some strongly assert reference to these "everlasting hills" means the Rocky Mountains. It's possible. Isaiah said that "in the last days, that the mountain of the Lord's house shall be established in the top of the mountains, and shall be exalted above the hills; and all nations shall flow unto it."[22] I would suggest it is not only a reference to the Church and temples being established in the Rocky Mountains.

A more modern revelation gives some other insights. We are exhorted to be steadfast and look forth "for the valleys to be exalted, and for the mountains to be made low, and for the rough places to become smooth. . . . Zion shall flourish upon the hills and rejoice upon the mountains, and shall be assembled together unto the place which I have appointed."[23] This seems to be a broad reference to Zion (the center place appointed and the stakes of Zion throughout the world). It is also reference as well to two distinct places—in the mountains and upon the hills.

There seems to be some geography we just don't fully understand. This is something to consider regarding "hills." At the time of the Flood, we have this topography tip: "And the waters prevailed exceedingly

---

20. Helaman 14:23.
21. D&C 133:25–34.
22. Isaiah 2:2.
23. See D&C 49:23–25.

upon the earth; and all the *high hills*, that were under the whole heaven, were covered. Fifteen cubits upward did the waters prevail; and the mountains were covered."[24] Are "high hills" and "mountains" one in the same? Again, sometimes in scripture, they probably are. Are the topographic extremes today exactly as they were before the Flood?

Habakkuk, in his trembling at the majesty of God, said: "He stood, and measured the earth: he beheld, and drove asunder the nations; and *the everlasting mountains were scattered*, the *perpetual hills* did bow: his ways are everlasting."[25] There is plenty of evidence in ecclesiastical history that confirms it isn't only the "dust of the earth [that moves] hither and thither, to the dividing asunder, at the command of our great and everlasting God. Yea, behold at his voice do the hills and the mountains tremble and quake."[26] Mountains and hills and all the waters obey His commands.

John the Revelator saw that during the sixth one-thousand-year period (sixth seal) of the earth's existence "every mountain and island [would be] moved out of their place" by a "great earthquake" that would cause a stark change in how we observe the lights in the firmament.[27] John also foresaw that an earthquake in the seventh one-thousand-year period (seventh seal) would be the most powerful "since men were upon the earth." He noted that "every island fled away and the mountains were not found."[28]

Topography (the landscape, scenery, and arrangement) and geography (description of the earth, including land features, climate, inhabitants) are something to consider now and possible anew as certain events unfold. So, what does this mean for the center place, the New Jerusalem?

---

24. Genesis 7:19. Italics for emphasis.
25. Habakkuk 3:6; italics for emphasis. Also consider Nahum 1:3–6.
26. Helaman 12:8–9.
27. Revelation 6:14. There are some that argue this earthquake has already happened. I do not think it has occurred yet.
28. Revelation 16:20. This mighty earthquake could be the same timing of the land masses coming back together. Again, see D&C 133:21–25.

If valleys will change and mountains be thrown down, why is Zion, the New Jerusalem, referred to as Mount Zion? Is a region currently with no distinct high peaks, and an elevation just under 1,000 feet a "mountain" or a "mount"? One possible view comes from Jay and Donald Parry's book *Understanding the Signs of the Times*: "Mount Zion is equated with the New Jerusalem. Why Mount? Because the gospel banner, or ensign, must be erected upon a high mountain for all nations to see. Mountains signify temples, and the temple[s] in New Jerusalem will be one of the great religious symbols of the holy city."[29] A dictionary in Joseph Smith's day defines mount as "a mass of earth, or earth and rock, rising considerably above the common surface of the surrounding land. Mount is used for an eminence or elevation of earth, indefinite in height or size, and may be a hillock, hill or mountain. A mound; a bulwark for offense or defense."[30] Such a definition brings us into harmony with scriptural references and context regarding Zion.

Let me provide you with some current particulars. Independence, Missouri, is almost 1,000 feet above sea level. Kansas City, Missouri, is about 900 feet above sea level. At certain spots in Independence, you can catch with the naked eye great views of downtown Kansas City. One spot is near the temple site designated by Joseph Smith.

But this elevation difference is miniscule to that of Mount Whitney in the Sierra Nevadas (just shy of 15,000 feet and the highest point in the continental United States), or to a place in Death Valley, which is about 280 below sea level. Remarkably, these two points of elevation are within 88 miles of each other (both in California). Yet, these places are unhabitable. You don't go there to build a home or

29. Jay A. Parry and Donald W. Parry, *Understanding the Signs of the Times*, 189.
30. *Noah Webster's 1828 Dictionary*, "Mount." Available online. With such definitions we can begin to see the spiritual meaning of Mount Zion. Jesus Christ mounting up Heavenly Father's ideals and ways. He is setting forth for all to see, glorious truths that will exalt all who will come and obey.

grow food or establish the foundations of a holy city. Have you ever been to Death Valley?

For elevation comparison, Salt Lake City sits more than 4,200 feet above sea level and Jerusalem of old nearly 2,500 feet above sea level. Do these elevation marks change when land is turned back into its place as it was before the earth was divided? There is scriptural evidence that Enoch built a city (though we don't know exactly where) amid a "land" that had "mountains" and "high places."[31] Regardless, there will still be variety to the earth. The topography of New Jerusalem should have plenty of admiring land marvels.

The earth will experience geography and topography adjustments. In some instances, big ones. We just can't grasp the adjustments coming. The magnificence and splendor of the earth will only improve as steps are taken to restore it to its paradisiacal glory. There is a perfection and a beauty unknown to our telestial eyes. Exactly what it will all look like is kept from us for now. When it is revealed, or when we live through the changes, geography and topography may become favorite subjects for many. Those who are upon the earth when these changes begin to occur will have reason to gather and marvel and wonder one with another.[32]

---

31. Study Moses 7:17–19.
32. 3 Nephi 11:1.

7

Stakes of Zion

"The Prophet Joseph intended that numerous new cities would be built as they filled up with faithful Saints in the 'stakes of Zion.'"[1]

We are not just talking about one city and one city only. Both New Jerusalem and Old Jerusalem will be flanked by stakes of Zion throughout the earth. Are these stakes also considered cities to some extent? Was there precedent established by first generation Latter-day Saints?

The Doctrine and Covenants identifies Kirtland, Far West, Nauvoo, and a stake that was to be west in the mountains. We know these were places of gathering. Though not mentioned as a stake in the Doctrine and Covenants, Adam-ondi-Ahman was established in this historical period when the Doctrine and Covenants was coming forth.

In addressing Kirtland as a *stake of Zion,* it doesn't get much clearer than this. The Lord said: "I have consecrated the land of Kirtland in

1. Richard Neitzel Holzapfel, "Establishing Zion in Preparation for the Second Coming," 112. In Robert L. Millet, editor. *Watch and Be Ready: Preparing for the Second Coming of the Lord,* 1994.

mine own due time for the benefit of the Saints of the Most High, and *for a stake of Zion*. For Zion must increase in beauty, and in holiness; her borders must be enlarged; her stakes must be strengthened; yea, verily I say unto you Zion must arise and put on her beautiful garments."[2]

Over a year later another revelation was received about this city-stake of Zion. Note that the Saints had already been gathering there for over two years. Yet the foundation of the city-stake had not officially been recognized. The Lord then identifies what they must do: "My friends, a commandment I give unto you, that ye shall commence a work of laying out and preparing a beginning and foundation of the city of the stake of Zion, here in the land of Kirtland, beginning at my house."[3]

The temple is once again brought to center attention. Temples will be essential and very apparent in these stakes of Zion. These early Saints in Kirtland were beginning a foundation. The Lord intends for the Kirtland stake to be a "strength of Zion," promising it should "be made strong."[4] There will be a temple again in Kirtland.[5] The original temple provided a setting for fasting, faith, learning, order, glory, and reflecting upon the House of God. The Lord will once again build up this area and city."[6] There is a Kirtland Stake organized today as constituted by current standards set by the presiding councils of the Church.

Far West was established in 1836. The organization of *the stake of Zion* in Far West happened on November 7, 1837. "The settlement in Far West was modeled after the 'Plat of the City of Zion,' a settlement plan originally intended for the building of Zion in Jackson County,

---

2. D&C 82:13–14.
3. D&C 94:1.
4. D&C 96:1.
5. Consider D&C 117:16. The historic Kirtland Temple owned by the Community of Christ Church is in the Lord's hands. Under their care, the Kirtland Temple has been preserved for many years. The Lord can identify other temples for this area, stake, and city.
6. D&C 124:83.

Missouri." Following a divine pattern, the temple was center stage as the foundation of the city. "On July 4, 1838, the Saints placed and dedicated the four cornerstones for a temple in their new city."[7]

Of this stake of Zion, the Lord emphasized to Saints arriving there in 1838: "Let the city, Far West, be a holy and consecrated land unto me; and it shall be called most holy, for the ground upon which thou standest is holy."[8] In the same revelation the emphasis continued: "And again, verily I say unto you, it is my will that the city of Far West should be built up speedily by the gathering of my Saints; And also that other places should be appointed for stakes in the regions round about, as they shall be manifested unto my servant Joseph, from time to time."[9] Though the stake and city never flourished in that decade, we have strong indications of it being reserved for another day.

There is a Far West Stake organized today as constituted by current standards set by the presiding councils of the Church. Adam-Ondi-Ahman is in the Far West Stake. "The Saints intended to build a city, establish a stake, and erect a temple in Adam-Ondi-Ahman as well. The City began to take shape and a stake was organized on June 28, 1838, but the temple was never formally started due to the persecutions."[10] There is plenty more to come in this region.

Nauvoo as *a stake in Zion* was highlighted in a January 1841 revelation. This is unique, because the Nauvoo Stake of Zion is referred to by the Lord as a "cornerstone of Zion."[11] With the Lord being very descriptive as to its course, He says that this stake "shall be polished with the refinement which is after the similitude of a palace."[12] Is there an intended distinction in referring to it as a

---

7. "Far West," Church history topics, https://www.churchofjesuschrist.org/study/history/topics/far-west?lang=eng.
8. D&C 115:7.
9. D&C 115:17–18.
10. Seminaries and Institutes of Religion publication, *Midwest Church History Workshop Guide.*
11. D&C 124:2, 23, 60, 131.
12. D&C 124:2, specifically.

"cornerstone"? One reputable author considered the original stake in the Salt Lake Valley another cornerstone.[13] Why?

One meaning of Nauvoo as a cornerstone stake could lean on the following: "In the early history of the Church a city-stake, Kirtland for instance, was laid out first and then the people came to live in it. Nauvoo was such a city-stake. A plan for the city was created and then people purchased lots and commenced to build up Zion, or the city. Thus, to say that Nauvoo is or was 'a cornerstone of Zion' is to say that the city was built according to the master plan by which all city-stakes were to be built."[14] This is, I believe, a beginning to comprehending Nauvoo Stake as a cornerstone of Zion. But there seems to be a bit more.

Nauvoo was purchased and laid out, and then Saints began to occupy lots and build it up. Given their experiences in Kirtland, Ohio, and Missouri, it is not surprising a temple lot was set aside. The leaders in Nauvoo had thought seriously on a piece of property. We know this, because in a revelation the Lord said, "Ye shall build it [the temple] on the place where you have contemplated building it, for that is the spot which I have chosen for you to build it."[15]

Nauvoo had modeled to a greater extent the building plan and establishment of a physical Zion. But Nauvoo was also the place where the Lord was revealing the spiritual blessings of the fulness of the priesthood. It wasn't just following a plat outline for a city. The Saints were instructed to "let [a] house be built unto my name, that I may reveal mine ordinances therein unto my people. For I deign to reveal unto my church things which have been hid from before the foundation of the world. . . . And I will show unto my servant Joseph all things pertaining to this house, and the priesthood therein."[16] There was much to come through the Lord's seer. This was to be

---

13. Glenn M. Leonard, *Nauvoo: A Place of Peace, A People of Promise*, 663.
14. Craig J. Ostler and Joseph Fielding McConkie. *Revelations of the Restoration*, 965–966.
15. D&C 124:43.
16. D&C 124:40–42.

"the beginning of the revelations and foundation of Zion, and for the glory, honor, and endowment of all her municipals, are ordained by the ordinance of my holy house."[17]

Municipals? What is inferred with this term? Hoyt W. Brewster explained, "The word *municipals*, as used in this sense, is probably akin to *municipalities*, which Webster defines as administrative areas having powers of local self-government. Therefore, municipals in this case undoubtedly has reference to the far-flung ecclesiastical units of the Church-branches, wards, districts, and stakes-which, while operating under the jurisdiction of the General Authorities, must function on a local basis."[18] I would agree with that statement, but may I suggest that municipals could also be about individuals themselves who want to live in a Zion community. Could it also be an endowment given to all those who carry out the civic affairs and responsibilities for Zion? The sacred formalities and teachings that are to come out of Zion, especially out of the house of Lord were intended to bless all people and all affairs in a covenant community situation.

During the last few years of Joseph Smith's life (in Nauvoo), he set forth all the ordinances and covenants of exaltation. A temple had to be erected for these to be acceptable. These ordinances and covenants were also set forth for the living and the dead. He organized women under priesthood keys, and these women began the Relief Society, an essential organization to the house of the Lord and the bringing forth of Zion. President Henry B. Eyring made this statement:

> You sisters, your daughters, your granddaughters, and the women you have nurtured will be at the heart of creating that society of people who will join in glorious association with the Savior. You will be an essential force in the gathering of Israel and in the creation of a Zion people who will dwell in peace in the New Jerusalem. The Lord has, through His prophets, made a promise

17. D&C 124:39.
18. Hoyt W. Brewster, *Doctrine and Covenants Encyclopedia*. See "municipals."

to you. In the early days of the Relief Society, the Prophet Joseph Smith said to the sisters, 'If you live up to your privileges, the angels cannot be restrained from being your associates.'[19]

Nauvoo can be considered a cornerstone stake because it had community ideal, a revealed civic plan, ecclesiastical structure even more so than before, and most important, it had a temple that offered the full endowment where individuals could receive every blessing pertaining to exaltation. This pattern seems to be acceptable to the Lord.[20] Therefore, the Nauvoo Stake could be called a cornerstone of Zion. It was a model or prototype. A pattern for future city-stakes yet to be created.

"Sunday, October 3, 1847, the Saints in the Salt Lake Valley met in conference and transacted business which had been proposed by President Young and the apostles. . . . 'Uncle' John Smith, who had been chosen before his arrival, was sustained as president of the Salt Lake Stake of Zion."

(Essentials in Church History, 379).

This brings us to the Great Basin. Salt Lake City and its numerous satellite communities were observed as *stakes of Zion*. At Winter Quarters, before the Saints pushed further west, Brigham Young received and recorded a revelation. The Rocky Mountains were ahead of them. The migrating Saints needed to establish a place of gathering to the west of those mountains. It was going to take everyone and their combined resources to establish *a stake of Zion*. The revelation given to President Young states: "Let every man use all his influence and property to remove this people to the place *where the Lord shall locate a stake of Zion*."[21]

19. "Sisters in Zion," *Ensign*, Nov. 2020.
20. Though the Saints vacated this community, there is a Nauvoo Stake organized today as constituted by current standards set by the presiding councils of the Church. Their temple was rebuilt and is an anchor to several surrounding stakes.
21. D&C 136:10.

The Lord, Brigham Young, and many others saw their westward expansion as a fulfillment of building up other stakes that would one day complement the center place of Zion. As early as 1831, the Lord was dropping hints that the expansion and buildup of the Church would be westward. This would hold "*until* . . . the city of the New Jerusalem shall be prepared."[22]

As Brigham Young and the people started to build up a community under Ensign Peak (a peak just north of downtown Salt Lake City), they saw the need and importance to begin other settlements. Hence, multiple stakes of Zion in the western United States began to flourish (south, west, north, and east of Salt Lake City)—all of them well over 1,000 miles from the land of Missouri and the place for Zion, the New Jerusalem. In the revelation received at Winter Quarters the Lord didn't revoke or ignore Zion in the center of the land. He stated, "Go thy way (west) and do as I have told you, and fear not thine enemies; for they shall not have power to stop my work. Zion shall be redeemed in mine own due time."[23]

It should be noted that where the Saints were camped in and near Winter Quarters (now Nebraska) is only 200 miles north (up the Missouri River Valley) from Independence, Missouri. Going south would have been a much more pleasant and a much shorter traveling experience than their westward efforts. You can see how many, in the genuineness of their hearts, wanted to try to redeem Zion.

We know some of the Latter-day Saints were reluctant to put much effort into building up a home in the mountains if it was only going to be temporary. I recall reading one time that some who had arrived in the Great Basin didn't feel inclined to move out of their wagons. They felt they would be going back to the land of Missouri soon. They had to be convinced to unpack their wagons. Those who couldn't be convinced went back east. In 1847 Winter Quarters was

22. D&C 42:8–9; italics for emphasis. See also D&C 45:64.
23. D&C 136:17–18.

temporary. Their stay in the mountains was not. The center place of Zion was put on hold. Ronald K. Esplin wrote:

> They had not forgotten that the center stake of Zion would one day be located in Jackson County, Missouri. (See D&C 57:1–3.) But the persecutions and tragedies of Missouri in the 1830s had made it plain that this center stake would not be established immediately. In fact, for the time being, the Lord had excused them from the commandment to build a temple there (see D&C 124:45–55) and had counseled them that Zion "shall be redeemed in mine own due time." (D&C 136:18.) Until then, they would have to find another home. . . . Someday the center stake of Zion, in Missouri, would be set in its proper place.[24]

These Saints who anticipated to go back very soon to Missouri can't be faulted for their eagerness. And they should be forgiven and not misjudged for their miscalculation of the Lord's timetable.[25] Several of them did stay and faithfully help set the foundations of multiple stakes

---

24. Ronald K. Esplin, "A 'Place Prepared' in the Rockies." Part of the series: *The Pioneers, Our Shared Heritage*. See *Ensign*, July 1988, 6–13. Brigham Young once stated: "You inquire if we shall stay in these mountains. I answer yes, as long as we please to do the will of God our Father in Heaven. If we are pleased to turn away from the holy commandments of the Lord Jesus Christ, as ancient Israel did, every man turning to his own way, we shall be scattered and peeled, driven before our enemies and persecuted, until we learn to remember the Lord our God and are willing to walk in his ways. Many may inquire, 'How long shall we stay here?' We shall stay here just as long as we ought to. 'Shall we be driven, when we go?' If we will so live as to be satisfied with ourselves, and will not drive ourselves from our homes we shall never be driven from them. Seek for the best wisdom you can obtain, learn how to apply your labor, build good houses, make fine farms, set out apple, pear, and other fruit trees that will flourish here, also the mountain currant and raspberry bushes, plant strawberry beds, and build up and adorn a beautiful city (*Discourses of Brigham Young*, 483–84).
25. See Elder Christofferson's remarks on early Saints who did not qualify to build the center place of Zion: "Rather than judge these early Saints too harshly, however, we should look to ourselves to see if we are doing any better." ("Come to Zion," *Ensign*, Nov. 2008).

of Zion in the west. Their struggles and achievements will not go unrecognized. Their doings and their devotion will be upon the records kept in the center place of Zion.[26] There are a whole host of lessons we can learn from them. President Lorenzo Snow summarized:

> Who cannot perceive the hand of God in bringing us from the turmoil and strife of the business world to these mountain vales, where we have the opportunity and the privilege of building up cities and villages upon the principle of unity which has been revealed to us, thus affording that necessary discipline which we could not have obtained among the cities of the Gentiles? This training cannot be acquired in one year, nor in five years, but its acquisition is enhanced in proportion to our willingness to sacrifice in order to obtain it. By and by the Lord will prepare the way for some to return to Jackson County, there to build up the metropolis of Zion. How easily this work can be accomplished, after we have learned to build up cities and temples here to His divine acceptance! Our present experience is a very needful one; without it we should be totally unfitted for the performance of such a work.[27]

Not only do we need to know how to plan and construct temples, but we need to know how to establish cities as well.[28] We need training. More training. And training after that. We need to know how to build communities and neighborhoods. We need to get experience in many things concerning construction, engineering, record keeping, printing (publishing in a variety of ways), education, global supply chain, mercantile, hard labor, and so on.

---

26. See D&C 69:1–6.
27. *Biography and Family Record of Lorenzo Snow*, 370–371.
28. Ibid. "As knowledge and efficiency are obtained gradually, we may expect that the experience we are getting now, in learning how to build up cities in our present condition—conforming as near as possible to the holy order of God, is designed to prepare us to return to Missouri, from whence we were driven, and there build up cities and temples to the name of the Most High, upon which His glory will descend. A condition of willingness to conform our will to the Divine will is what we need" (371).

Think on that. We have a lot of lessons to learn. As a people and a divine institution, our reservoir of knowledge concerning this concept steadily increases. Great sacrifice is before us. A capital city is before us.

Until the center place arrives, we need to help the current stakes of Zion that are being placed and anchored to support a holy and glorious part of the tent. As we consider the importance of these stakes of Zion, we need to remember that Joseph Smith saw a much broader vision of the concept of Zion. "In the spring of 1844, Joseph Smith emphasized . . . 'all of North and South America is Zion.'" And at His last general conference of the Church, he declared that "they could build up churches throughout the continent until 'all Zion is built up.' As the Prophet had foreseen, eventually Zion would fill all of North and South America."[29] How? By satellite cities and communities flanked with temples and individuals living as a Zion people.

Joseph Smith and all his contemporary Saints had at least four practice runs establishing a stake of Zion. By the time the Saints set up the initial stake in Salt Lake City, the practicing was over. The Lord had given the cornerstone example (city-stake of Nauvoo) and set the foundation. The growing Church and faithful people had something to go on. They now would begin replicating the concept over and over.

One author noted: "For nearly sixty years, gathering to Utah and to other Latter-day Saint settlements in Canada, Mexico, Colorado, Arizona, Idaho, Wyoming, and Nevada still remained a high priority for Church leaders. This changed, however, during the beginning of the twentieth century partly because of economic and political events in the United States. Yet the Brethren saw the hand of the Lord in these events and began to unfold a much larger view of the Latter-day

---

29. Ronald K. Esplin, "A 'Place Prepared' in the Rockies." Part of the series "The Pioneers, Our Shared Heritage." See *Ensign*, July 1988, 6–13. "Unfortunately, this statement does not give more specific details on the size and expanse of the New Jerusalem. Joseph Smith later announced that 'the whole of America is Zion itself from north to south.' But what his declaration meant in regard to the size of the New Jerusalem, as a great complex of cities of Zion, was not made clear" (Hyrum L. Andrus, *Doctrines of the Kingdom*, 298).

Saints' responsibility of establishing stakes of Zion throughout the world."[30] Even recently prophets have encouraged individuals and families to gather in the nations "in each realm where He has given His Saints their birth and nationality."[31] Hence the creation of thousands of stakes since the days of Brigham Young's administration.

The New Jerusalem will be flanked by multiplying stakes (cities) of Zion.[32] The concept of Zion, as it unfolds, will not only be powerful but contagious. It will flood places of the earth and those places and its inhabitants will blossom.

President Russell M. Nelson said, "Spiritual security will always depend upon *how* one lives, not *where* one lives. I promise that if we will do our best to exercise faith in Jesus Christ and access the power of His atonement through repentance, we will have the knowledge and power of God to help us take the blessings of the restored gospel

---

30. Richard Neitzel Holzapfel, "Establishing Zion in Preparation for the Second Coming," 122. In Robert L. Millet, editor. *Watch and Be Ready: Preparing for the Second Coming of the Lord*, 1994.
31. "The Future of the Church," *Ensign*, April 2020, 15.
32. I do believe it worth mentioning here that Martha Jane Knowlton Coray reported a sermon Joseph Smith gave in July of 1840. Part of her report states that in his sermon Joseph referenced the parable of the nobleman and his very choice spot of land (see D&C 101:43–62). Specifically, Joseph referenced the planting of "twelve olive trees" (see v. 44). Some of her report of Joseph Smith's sermon reads: "The Land of Zion . . . consisted of all N. & S America but that any place where the Saints gather is Zion which every righteous man will build up for a place of safety for his children [and] that The olive trees are 12 stakes which are yet to be built not the Temple in Jackson as some suppose. For while the 12 olive stakes are being built we will be at peace but the Nations of the Earth will be at war. . . .

    "The redemption of Zion is the redemption of all N & S America and those 12 stake must be built up before the redemption of Zion can take place and those who refuse to gather and build when they are commanded to do so cease to be Saviours of men and are thenceforth good for nothing but shall be cast out and trodden underfeet of men" See *Jospeh Smith Papers website*: JS, Discourse, Nauvoo, Hancock Co., IL, ca. 19 July 1840. Featured version copied [between fall 1843 and 1850s] in Martha Jane Coray, Notebook, ca. 1843–1850s, [9]–[22]; handwriting of Martha Jane Knowlton Coray; CHL.

of Jesus Christ to every nation, kindred, tongue, and people and to prepare the world for the Second Coming of the Lord."[33]

I give the following observation as my opinion. There may yet be further cities established by Latter-day Saints—stakes of Zion. Scriptural precedence provides some examples of other covenant driven people doing the same thing. For example, the Nephites, for strategic and security reasons, set "the foundation" for at least four new cities (though it says many) during Captain Moroni's days.[34] We know the surviving Nephites at the time of the Savior's visit rebuilt (or renewed) cities that were destroyed.[35] As cities experience their own interruptions and desolations, we will see demographic adjustments with Latter-day Saints.

With this in mind, it could be observed that current stake geographical boundaries are fluid. It seems that stake geographical boundaries and the measures by which they are created and sustained today may broaden in concept with time. In some instances, those geographical boundaries may get smaller, in some instances larger. They will ebb and flow as events continue to unfold. For Saints to have refuge and protection along with access to resources and sociality, some individuals and families may have to adjust and relocate. Unforeseen events can change physical situations and demographics relatively quickly.[36]

---

33. "The Future of the Church." *Ensign*, April 2020, 16.
34. See Alma 50:13–15.
35. See 4 Nephi 1:7–9.
36. Again, consider footnote 32 of this chapter. One example could be what happened after Hurricane Katrina in 2005. The destruction caused many Latter-day Saints to relocate out of the region. The Slidell Louisiana Stake was devastated. "The LDS population decreased to a point that the number of stakes operating in the hurricane-impacted region could not be maintained. Church leaders decided to dissolve the Slidell Louisiana Stake and reapportion its units across several surrounding stakes." Ten years later the Church reestablished the Slidell Louisiana Stake ("Elder Christofferson Reorganizes Same Louisiana Stake He Dissolved after Hurricane Katrina," *Church News,* November 7, 2017. https://www.churchofjesuschrist.org/church/news/elder-christofferson-reorganizes-same-louisiana-stake-he-dissolved-after-hurricane-katrina?lang=eng).

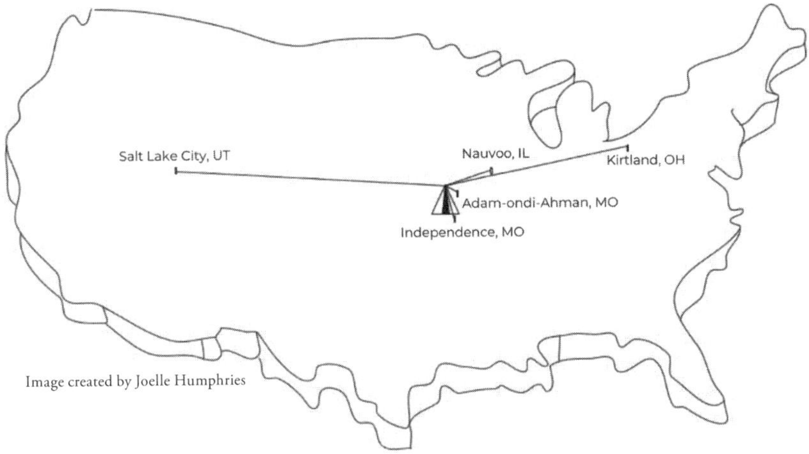

Image created by Joelle Humphries

Temples will be an integral part of this adjustment. Gathering near those temples in proximity may be crucial. President Nelson has brought attention to the lopsidedness with chapels and temples: "The only buildings that are absolutely essential are temples. Stake centers and chapels are a luxury. This imbalance is on our worry list. . . . Faith, repentance, baptism, the endowment, and the sealing ordinance are essential. Everything you'll see happening in the Church from this point forward will be in that direction."[37]

It is up to each of us to align with that direction and "seek to bring forth and establish the cause of Zion."[38]

---

37. Sheri Dew, Sheri. *Insights*, 405–406.
38. D&C 12:6.

8

The Sovereignty of Zion

"Social peace and political stability will prevail over the whole earth as all humanity will be one large community under the sovereignty of Jesus Christ."[1]

It is Jesus Christ's right to reign.[2] So how do we get there? How will we get there? Perhaps a simple and direct revelation by the Prophet Joseph Smith, on April 25, 1844, gets to the point: "Verily thus saith the Lord, ye are my constitution and I am your God, and ye are my spokesmen. From henceforth do as I shall command you. Saith the Lord."[3]

Who are the "spokesmen" referred to in this revelation? What is the context of this revelation?

Months before and days leading up to his martyrdom, Joseph Smith had gathered a select group of men. He wanted to set forth

1. Victor L. Ludlow, *Principles and Practices of the Restored Gospel*, 629.
2. D&C 58:22.
3. See Gerrit Dirkmaat and Andrew C. Reed, "The Kingdom of God and His Laws," in *How and What You Worship* [the 49th Annual Brigham Young University Sidney B. Sperry Symposium], 295.

the kingdom of God on earth governed by a body that would become known as the "Council of Fifty."[4] This kingdom of God would "protect the members of the Church in their freedom to worship as they chose, but it would also protect those who wanted to worship God and Christ in their own way."[5] The Council wanted to end religious persecution they and others were experiencing. They wanted independence, dominion, autonomy, power, and freedom—this is sovereignty. The Lord desires each to live in such a setting. The gift of agency craves such a setting. "Prophecy told" this council "an independent kingdom would be established before the Second Coming, and this was the moment."[6]

It was this council that "was tasked with planning and preparing a constitution for this new government, a kingdom that would await the imminent return of Jesus Christ, who would then assume his rightful place at the head of that kingdom."[7] Why a new government? The United States government, in the Saints' opinion, had failed them. Governments all over the world were failing. They were given to cruelty, bloodshed, carnage, pride, corruption, impurity, intrigue, spiritual wickedness in high places, party factions, and so on.[8]

In 1842, a Church periodical published an article titled "The Government of God." According to Derek R. Sainsbury, "The article asked, 'Where is there a man that can step forth and alter the destiny of nations and promote the happiness of the world?' The

---

4. The official name given by Joseph Smith under inspiration was "The Kingdom of God and his Laws, with the keys and power therof, and the judgement in the hands of his servants. Ahman Christ" (Ibid., 280).
5. Ibid., 290.
6. Richard Lyman Bushman, "The Separatist Impulse in the Nauvoo Council of Fifty," in *The Council of Fifty: What the Records Reveal about Mormon History,* [Matthew J. Grow and R. Eric Smith, eds.], 1.
7. See Gerrit Dirkmaat and Andrew C. Reed, "The Kingdom of God and His Laws," 271.
8. See Nathan B. Oman, "We, the People of the Kingdom of God: Constitution Writing in the Council of Fifty," in *The Council of Fifty: What the Records Reveal about Mormon History* [Matthew J. Grow and R. Eric Smith, eds.], 62.

answer was the government of God: 'It has been the design of Jehovah, from the commencement of the world, and is his purpose now. To regulate the affairs of the world in his own time . . . and take the reins of government into his own hand.'"[9]

Joseph Smith sought to prepare a governing body that would provide and protect the temporal salvation of all people, not just Latter-day Saints. For this to happen he wanted to see aristarchy and theodemocracy prevail. Not to be confused with aristocracy, *aristarchy* refers to good men in power or government discharged by excellent men who are honest and wise. *Theodemocracy* was defined and sustained by Joseph Smith in the context of "God's government [that] existed with the patriarchs. . . . 'They had God to make their laws, and men chosen by him to administer them . . . in both civil and ecclesiastical affairs; they were both one . . . ; So will it be when the purposes of God shall be accomplished.'"[10]

Lots of open land to the west beckoned the Saints. At the time, much of it was not under the United States sovereignty. The westward regions are where this council intended to establish their governance and do so by the "government of God."[11] However, the land in the west wasn't going to be available for long. America's borders from sea to shining sea was just about complete. The Oregon

---

9. Derek R. Sainsbury, *Storming the Nation: The Unknown Contributions of Joseph Smith's Missionaries*, 20.
10. Ibid., 20. Many LDS scholars have addressed these words and Joseph Smith's views on government in his day and God's government in the last days. Another way to define theodemocracy is "where God and the people hold the power to conduct the affairs of men in righteousness" (see page 17 of Sainsbury's book). This concept of men being governed as they were in the days of patriarchs is confirmed by this simple statement in Moses 6:7: "Now this same priesthood, which was in beginning, shall be in the end of world also."
11. Richard Lyman Bushman, "The Separatist Impulse in the Nauvoo Council of Fifty," in *The Council of Fifty: What the Records Reveal about Mormon History,* [Matthew J. Grow and R. Eric Smith, eds.], 3. Brigham Young said in May 1845, "When we go from here [Nauvoo] we don't' calculate to go under any government but the government of God."

territory was settled in 1846, and the Mexican Cessation happened in 1848. In retrospect, the efforts of this original Council of Fifty can be understood as foundational, much like the original Saints who went to Jackson County in 1831 to establish Zion.

Initially a few men were tasked with writing a constitution for this body to govern. They were terribly unsuccessful and admitted it was so.[12] They wanted the Prophet Joseph Smith to be added to this writing committee. He declined and argued that the Council had to obtain secular knowledge and inspiration. Prophetic counsel could clarify, correct, and redirect after individuals and the council collective did their own work of study and information gathering. He held the notion that "if the council simply relied on [him] to tell them what to do, they would not increase their own abilities."[13] This is something to keep in mind in our day as events unfold and governments collapse.

Practical Brigham Young didn't hold his tongue in these Council of Fifty meetings. He wanted no lengthy or heavily worded constitution. It was appalling to him to mimic what nations and governments of his day had done and were doing. "To Young, The Church and the kingdom of God were so distinct from the rest of the world that they could not be compared. 'Revelations must govern. The voice of God shall be the voice of the people.'"[14] Of course, this aligns with Joseph Smith's aristarchy and theodemocracy ideas.

Brigham Young must have been pleased when he heard the simple and direct revelation that served as the Council of Fifty's constitution: "Verily thus saith the Lord, ye are my constitution and I am your God, and ye are my spokesmen. From henceforth do as I shall command you. Saith the Lord."[15] Compare those

12. Willard Richards, John Taylor, and W.W. Phelps were draft committee members.
13. See Gerrit Dirkmaat and Andrew C. Reed, "The Kingdom of God and His Laws." In Rachel Cope, Carter Charles, and Jordan T. Watkins, eds. *How and What You Worship*, 283–284.
14. Ibid., 295.
15. Ibid.

thirty words with most constitutions in the world (which range from 3,000 to 15,000 words). I can understand Brigham's not wanting to compare them.

One important scriptural and doctrinal distinction that has been clarified with the release of the *Joseph Smith Papers* is the understanding of the term "the kingdom of God." For years we have referred to The Church of Jesus Christ of Latter-day Saints solely as the kingdom of God on earth. And rightly so, especially when we contemplate what Joseph Smith had communicated to him by the Lord in October of 1831. "The keys of the kingdom of God are committed unto man on the earth, and from thence shall the gospel roll forth unto the ends of the earth, as the stone which is cut out of the mountain without hands shall roll forth, until it has filled the whole earth. . . . Wherefore, may the kingdom of god go forth."[16] Without argument, there is a strong connection that the gospel is part of the kingdom of God.

The kingdom of God cannot operate or be built up unless Jesus Christ extends keys to His presiding high priest. This has happened. As the Lord gave them, Joseph Smith revealed the kingdom of God line upon line. However, he called upon others and didn't try to take the reins as a dictator as some accused him doing. If we are going to get to aristarchy and theodemocracy, the Lord's presiding key holder will have to be somewhat in the mix. "The gifts of prophets, evangelists &c," Joseph Smith observed, "never were designed to govern men in civil matters. The kingdom of God has nothing to do with giving commandments to damn a man spiritually. It only has power to make a man amenable to his fellow man. . . . In relation to the constitution of the United States, there is but one difficulty, and that is, the constitution provides the things which we want but lacks the power to carry the laws into effect. We want to alter it so as to make it imperative on the officers to enforce the protection of all men in their rights."[17]

---

16. D&C 65 2, 6. Read the entirety of the section for clarity.
17. Council of Fifty, Minutes, Nauvoo, Hancock Co., IL, 18 Apr. 1844; in Council of Fifty, "Record," [142]–[206]; handwriting of William Clayton; CHL. Accessed 14 January 2021.

> "We act upon the broad and liberal principle that all men have equal rights, and ought to be respected, and that every man has a privilege in this organization [Council of Fifty] of choosing for himself voluntarily his God, and what he pleases for his religion, inasmuch as there is no danger but that every man will embrace the greatest light. God cannot save or damn a man only on the principle that every man acts, chooses and worships for himself; hence the importance of thrusting from us every spirit of bigotry and intolerance towards a man's religious sentiments. . . . Intolerance and bigotry never had a place in this kingdom, nor in my breast. . . . Nothing can reclaim the human mind from its ignorance, bigotry, superstition &c but those grand and sublime principles of equal rights and universal freedom to all men."
>
> —Joseph Smith
>
> (Joseph Smith Statement April 11, 1844, Council of Fifty Minutes)

Many other good people will help anchor not only the Church, but the forthcoming aspects of the political kingdom—the kingdom of God.

Late in his life as the subject matured in his mind, Joseph taught, "There is a distinction between the Church of God and the kingdom of God. The laws of the kingdom are not designed to effect our salvation hereafter. It is an entire, distinct and separate government. . . . The Church is a spiritual matter and a spiritual kingdom, but the kingdom which Daniel saw was not a spiritual kingdom; but was designed to be got up for the safety and salvation of the Saints by protecting them in their religious rights and worship."[18] Is there a distinction between the Church of God and the kingdom of God? Yes. Are they exclusively independent of one another? No. Both will fill the earth. Daniel's "dream is certain, and the interpretation thereof sure."[19]

18. Ibid.
19. Daniel 2:35, 45.

The Church of God and the kingdom of God on earth will be set for the establishment of Zion. Our temple worship not only accentuates the order of restoration, but also the three distinctions. Three distinctions—yes. Exclusively independent of one another—no. There will be a marvelous blend as situations and events continue to unfold.

As we consider this distinction and the solidarity of the Church of God and the kingdom of God, we can begin to put into better context Joseph's prophecies that the "elders of Israel" and "this people" [the Latter-day Saints] will one day help sustain and save the constitution of the United States. One reliable source, Eliza R. Snow, said: "I heard the prophet Joseph Smith say . . . that the time would come when this nation would so far depart from its original purity, its glory, and its love for freedom and its protection of civil and religious rights, that the Constitution of our country would hang as it were by a thread. He said, also, that this people, the sons of Zion, would rise up and save the Constitution and bear it off triumphantly."[20]

Let's put ourselves into the revelations that tell us where this church and kingdom are headed. In 1830, the Lord told us the condition for His Saints when He comes: "I have made the earth. . . . It is my footstool, wherefore, again I will stand upon it. And I hold forth and deign to give unto you greater riches, even a land of promise. . . . And I will give it unto you for the land of your inheritance. . . . In time ye shall have no king nor ruler, for I will be your king and watch over you. Wherefore, hear my voice and follow me, and you shall be a free people, and ye shall have no laws but my laws when I come, for I am your lawgiver, and what can stay my hand?[21]

He asks a great question: "What can stay [His] hand?" We ought to ponder it.

---

20. Valletta, *Great American Documents for Latter-Day Saint Families*, 47. See also *Deseret News Weekly*, 556. Brigham Young and Orson Pratt (and others) have documented such language and prophecy from Joseph Smith as well.
21. See D&C 38:17–22.

In our view, when we read and study about Joseph Smith trying to establish the kingdom of God and the Council of Fifty among the Saints, we may see "much of their rhetoric [as] froth, not hard policy. But they gave vent repeatedly and passionately. Beneath their appeals for a refuge lay a deep anger."[22] The rights were being trampled. They were being governed by what they saw as corrupt individuals far removed from the Lord. They sought the laws of Jesus Christ to govern their existence and honor their agency.

Other revelations supported what they were hoping to accomplish. "Be subject to the powers that be, until he reigns whose right it is to reign, and subdues all enemies under his feet," the Lord declared. Knowing what we know, that God will reign personally upon the earth, can you fault early Saints being impatient with the powers by which they were being governed and by which they were being abused? The following words are: "Behold, the laws which ye have receive from my hand are the laws of the church, and in this light ye shall hold them forth. Behold, here is wisdom."[23]

President Russell M. Nelson reminded us that the Restoration is ongoing. I do not think it is a stretch to submit that further revelations will help set forth laws pertaining to the kingdom of God and laws by which His people and others will be governed.[24] But before that will happen the Lord emphasized: "But first let my army become very great, and let it be sanctified before me, that it may become fair as the sun, and clear as the moon, and that her banners may be terrible unto all nations; that the kingdoms of this world may be constrained to acknowledge that the kingdom of Zion is in

---

22. Richard Lyman Bushman, "The Separatist Impulse in the Nauvoo Council of Fifty," in *The Council of Fifty: What the Records Reveal about Mormon History,* [Matthew J. Grow and R. Eric Smith, eds.], 2.

23. D&C 58:22–23.

24. In the meantime, the Lord feels it necessary that we "hasten to translate [His] scriptures, and to obtain a knowledge of history, and of countries, and of kingdoms, of laws of God and man, and all this for the salvation of Zion" (see D&C 93:53.)

very deed the kingdom of our God and his Christ; therefore, let us become subject unto her laws.[25]

The kingdom of Zion, the holy city of New Jerusalem, will eventually have her sovereignty. She will be supported by the kingdom of God. She will not be under the iron, brass, clay, silver, and gold hand of ungodly nations governed by Satan's political puppets and dictators. "The wind" Daniel foresaw would "[carry] them away."[26]

But getting to that point isn't going to be without serious trouble. John's revelation about the "woman" [the Church of God] and the "man child" [kingdom of our God and his Christ] was set in the imagery of woman giving birth. She was "travailing in birth, and pained to be delivered." In her agony and distress she beheld Satan and his host standing before her "to devour her child as soon as it was born."[27]

Do you see what we are up against? Put this book down and think on that for a minute.

John's account favorably concludes that the woman [the Church of God] did safely deliver the man child [kingdom of our God and his Christ] and "her child was caught up unto God, and to his throne."[28] It ends triumphantly. But the labor pains have just started.

The prosperity, intrigue, corruption, and collapse of government as told in the Book of Mormon provide us a prescient view of what is to come. And unfortunately, it puts a great stress on the Church.[29] Gerald Lund wrote, "Think of the king-men versus the freemen, the Gadianton robbers versus the elected government, and finally the total collapse of the government when Gadianton robbers seized full power. These example may serve as types or shadows of things that are to come."[30]

25. D&C 105:31–32. Also consider Revelation 11:15.
26. Daniel 2:35.
27. Revelation 12:1–6. It would be more helpful to read JST, Revelation 12:1–7.
28. Ponder and study Revelation 12:1–6.
29. I would encourage the reader to study 3 Nephi 3–7 (note in particular 6:13–14; 7:6).
30. Gerald N. Lund, *The Second Coming of the Lord*, 174.

We are called upon to help *deliver* the kingdom of God. To do this, we must understand and sustain moral law. We must sustain and honor laws that are "framed and held inviolate as will secure to each individual the free exercise of conscience, the right to control property, and the protection of life."[31] We are called, individually, and collectively as a church, to hold the laws of God forth, as a light, unto all. The Church of Jesus Christ of Latter-day Saints has wonderful "banners" (standards) that can and will bless the peaceful people of the earth, even when they refuse or are indifferent to the covenant path taught through temple worship.

To begin to sum up this chapter consider the words of John Taylor:

> The kingdom of God [will] be literally established on the earth. . . . The Lord will be king over all the earth, and all mankind literally under his sovereignty, and every nation under the heavens will have to acknowledge his authority, and bow to his sceptre. Those who serve him in righteousness will have communications with God, and with Jesus; will have the ministering of Angels, and will know the past, the present, and the future; and other people, who may not yield full obedience to his laws, nor be fully instructed in his covenants, will, nevertheless, have to yield full obedience to his government. . . .
>
> Satan will not then be permitted to control its inhabitants, for the Lord God will be king over all the earth, and the kingdom and greatness of the kingdom under the whole heaven will be given to the Saints. . . . Satan has had his dominion, and has deceived, corrupted, and cursed the human family; but then his dominion will be destroyed, and he will be cast into the bottomless pit. . . . The fear of God, and the observance of his laws, will be looked upon in their proper light. God will be seen, feared, and worshipped as our Father, Friend, and Benefactor; his laws will be kept as being those framed by infinite wisdom, and the most conducive to the happiness of the human family. Virtue,

31. D&C 134:2. Read the section in its entirety.

> truth, and righteousness, will appear in their native loveliness, beauty, simplicity, glory, and magnificence, for God alone will be exalted in that day.
>
> How will the kingdom of God be established? . . . None of the means which are now used among men are commensurate with the object designed, and that all the combined wisdom of man must, and will fail, in the accomplishment of this object; that the present forms of political and religious rule cannot effect it; that philosophy is quite as impotent; and that as these have all failed for ages, as a natural consequence they must continue to fail. . . . But God can put it right.[32]

With the help of His Father, Our Savior, Jesus Christ, can put it right. If He created the earth, He can subdue it. He will support the woman [His Church] in travail. His purposes and millennial reign can't be overthrown by any wicked coup. He is preparing a nursery (or nurseries) for the man child [His kingdom]—Zion and her stakes.

Because of the prophesied location of the center place of Zion (the New Jerusalem), I submit all eyes are on America. She is currently in confusion. There are ominous clouds on the horizon. Some are gloating in this, others are terribly saddened, still others are frustrated and angry.

In revolutionary rhetoric, patriot Thomas Paine wrote, "These are the times that try men's souls."[33] Calamitous political events of our day resurrect these words. As ancient and modern scripture attest, "all things shall be in commotion and surely men's hearts shall fail them."[34] Ours is a day when some events are hard to understand. People don't readily see when their liberty, life, and property are being threatened, or are even taken right before their eyes. Ours is a day when individuals don't understand their right to exercise of conscience. This, in many ways, is because they have seared their conscience "with a hot iron."[35]

---

32. *Government of God*, 87–88.
33. *The American Reader: Words that Moved a Nation* (1991), 28.
34. D&C 88:91.
35. 1 Timothy 4:2.

This is where sin has led us. Sin erodes divine knowledge. A lack of understanding, further deception, and indifference are the artificial pillars of a sinful life. For some it turns into rebellion. Vile rebellion. Current events provide ample evidence of this. Such artificial pillars can't hold. They will crumble. What is threatened? Individual, community, state, and national sovereignty is threatened. What will fill the void?

In the spring of 1776 at the siege of Boston, George Washington positioned his troops to take Dorchester Heights. To inspire his officers, he said, "As the season is now fast approaching when every man must expect to be drawn into the field of action, it is highly necessary that he should prepare his mind, as well as everything necessary for it. It is a noble cause we are engaged in; it is the cause of virtue and mankind."[36] Insightful and prophetic, this aligns with and has a beautiful rhyme to words that will inspire people to seek and build up Zion.

The noble cause of virtue beckons America to forthright introspection, individually and collectively. For well over 200 years, the people of all nations have been beneficiaries of America's generosity. They have noted her inventions and followed her educational endeavors. They have benefited from these inventions and relied on her commerce and industry. They have been blessed by her resources and inspired by her religions. They have been protected by her military and tutored by her government. They have noted the strength of her families and studied the faith of her fathers.

The whole world has America in sight. "The United States Constitution," President Dallin H. Oaks points out, "is the oldest written constitution still in force today. Though originally adopted by

36. David McCullough, *1776*, 91. John Adams spoke of the virtue needed to sustain ourselves as a people. "The only foundation of a free Constitution is pure virtue, and if this cannot be inspired into our people in a greater measure than they have it now, they may change their rulers and the forms of government, but they will not obtain lasting liberty. They will only exchange tyrants for tyrannies." See *Our Sacred Honor* (William J. Bennett), 371.

only a small number of colonies, it soon became a model worldwide. Today, every nation except three have adopted written constitutions."[37] Again, the whole world has America in sight. Even the caustic led nations of tyranny and oppression, at minimum (we could even argue with great interest), maintain a peripheral interest in America's unfolding destiny.

The climax of that unfolding destiny is the coming New Jerusalem.

The Constitution of the United States sustains moral agency if moral representatives and a moral citizenry all uphold moral law. What America will become in the twenty-first century depends not only on how faithfully we befriend the constitutional law of the land collectively, but what we become individually. The victory will be in private virtue.

I submit that those who walk in virtue will be upheld by the Lord's power. Those who honor covenants with Him will succeed in the "field of action." This is the army in which millions of God's children desire to enlist. Virtuous citizens are good neighbors. Active and engaged neighbors help and serve others. They are also driven to sustain a strong nuclear family. This is time consuming and rarely convenient. Perhaps it's time for more of them (of us) to come out of the political shade.[38]

Before disembarking on sacred soil (soil they believed would eventually yield Zion the New Jerusalem), Plymouth colonizers began the Mayflower Compact with these words: "In the name of God, Amen." They agreed to "covenant and combine ourselves together into a civil body politic, for our better ordering and preservation . . . which we promise all due submission and obedience." When did people stop asking submission and obedience to whom?

Circus-tent politics and beauty-pageant Christianity are not the answer for the challenges we face and the solutions we need. We have, as the ancient seer said, "put no difference between the holy

37. "Defending Our Divinely Inspired Constitution," *Liahona*, May 2021.
38. John Adams held that some of the "best political plants grow in the shade" (Rodney K. Smith, *James Madison: The Father of Religious Liberty*, 372).

and profane, neither have they showed difference between unclean and the clean" (Ezekiel 22:26). Our cowardice to admit what is wrong is speeding the decline of not only misery but our personal and collective sovereignty.

We are, in many ways a disobedient people. The political chaos, the domestic destructions, the lawlessness, and the terribly sad state of our families confirm this. "If righteousness exalteth a nation" (Proverbs 14:34), what does disobedience or wickedness do? It leads to bondage over and over and over.

When Ezekiel had to confront Jerusalem in its decadence, he conveyed for the Lord that a man was sought for to "make up the hedge, and stand in the gap (the breach) before me (Jesus Christ) for the land, that I should not destroy it: but I found none."[39]

I don't think this is our lot today. I think Jesus Christ has men and women, already here and soon to be coming into mortality, who will yet form the hedge and stand in the gap for Him. "There shall be a day," Jeremiah prophesied, "that the watchman upon the mount Ephraim shall cry, Arise ye, and let us go up to Zion unto the Lord our God."[40] That day is close at hand.

Zion will have its sovereignty. Zion will stop the breach. The Lord will sustain the hedge. We ought to look for and uphold those who understand this.

---

39. Ezekiel 22:30.
40. Jeremiah 31:6.

9

3 Nephi 3—A Forecast

"We will prepare ourselves in the center of our lands."[1]

Zion, the new Jerusalem, is an everlasting ideal that leads to a oneness and perfection. It is a people. It involves geography and physical places of gathering. As alluded to in chapters 5 and 6, there are many factors that can cause severe disruptions that require people to relocate, to gather somewhere else (Mother Nature, war, domestic turmoil, and economic downfalls).

What can we expect to be up against as Jesus Christ sets in order Zion, the center place? As we considered Zion, the New Jerusalem, in the center of the land, are there any relevant lessons from 3 Nephi 3? Why did a people described in the Book of Mormon gather in the center of the land for over seven years? Are the circumstances that led them to gather a type of what we may expect and experience?

To thwart off their enemies that were threatening their destruction, the Nephites gathered "unto one place."[2] The "band of robbers,"

1. 3 Nephi 3:21
2. 3 Nephi 3:13.

or the Gadianton robbers, had "become so numerous, and did slay so many of the people, and did lay waste so many cities, and did spread so much death and carnage throughout the land, that it became expedient that all the people, both the Nephites and the Lamanites, should take up arms against them."[3]

The unification of the Lamanites and Nephites expediently occurred as to protect their wives and children and to preserve their privileges of worship, individual freedoms, and collective liberty.[4] War was thrust upon them by an aggressive enemy who threatened these privileges and their very lives. With much effort and toil, they drove the Gadianton robbers out of their lands for a season.

We must note that war and civil unrest preceded the governor's proclamation to gather in the center of the lands. In our day ominous clouds forecast the same trend. Unless we repent, these clouds will bring a severe storm. Mormon didn't hide the prevailing issue with the unified Nephites. "Because of the wickedness of the people of Nephi," he said they lost many advantages and instead had to shoulder many afflictions. "The sword of destruction" hung over them.[5]

Justice, in this case, wasn't on their side anyway. If they weren't fighting with the robbers, they were contending amongst themselves. The proclamation to gather softened their hearts enough to work out their temporal and physical salvation another way. It was time to put down the sword and do their best to return to the Lord.

The leader of the robbers, Giddianhi, in his pride was unaware of the divine intervention about to be extended to the Nephites. Fortunately, the Nephites had wise leaders in their midst. "In [3 Nephi 3] we are able to witness a stark contrast. On the one hand we find the bold and egotistical Giddianhi, the Gadianton leader who demands a Nephite surrender. On the other hand we see the quiet and righteous confidence of Lachoneus and Gidgiddoni,

---

3. 3 Nephi 2:11.
4. 3 Nephi 2:12.
5. 3 Nephi 2:18–19.

the humble Nephite leaders who know absolutely from whence true strength comes."[6] Their rational and bold approach to the situation helped derail Giddianhi and his followers.

There are plenty of individuals in our day like unto egotistical Giddianhi. Consider some stinging details Mormon's account gives. More accurately, it is straight from the words of Giddianhi himself. Mormon had access to an epistle Giddianhi had sent a Nephite chief governor named Lachoneus. It is telling, especially if we want to understand how those in secret and corrupt societies work. His epistles can be found in 3 Nephi 3:2–10. Gidiannhi's letter reveals:

1. Those in secret societies are given to flattery. They pretend to praise and appreciate the firmness and steadfastness of the faithful. Yet, they secretly despise the faithful and desire to strip liberty from them and in some istances, destory them. (3 Nephi 3:2)
2. In another breath, they use scare tactics and make threats. They talk down to the righteous and try to convince them how "foolish and vain" they are to put their faith and trust in God and not in the hand of a government or authoritarian power. (3 Nephi 3:3)
3. They pretend to feel for your welfare or have deep concern for life. They don't. They kill and have a superficial respect for human life. They gloat in public about caring and about saving lives, but they destroy others' lives in secret. (3 Nephi 3:5)
4. They demand that certain people, whom they designate as the privileged, to yield up their cities, lands, possessions, and substance. (3 Nephi 3:6, 10)
5. They want others to join in their corruption. Their appeals sometimes happen secretly and sometimes in broad daylight. They want others to develop their attitude of nobility or elitism. These are shallow promises. (3 Nephi 3:7)

---

6. Joseph Fielding McConkie and Robert Millet, *Doctrinal Commentary on the Book of Mormon*, vol. 4:15.

6. They refer to their collective darkness as a brotherhood and want to control and ruin those who refuse to accept or be part of their works of wickedness. (3 Nephi 3:7–8)
7. They know they are a secret society. Their approach fulfills Isaiah's words: "Woe unto them who call evil good, and good evil; that put darkness for light, and light for darkness; that put bitter for sweet, and sweet for bitter." (Isaiah 5:20; 3 Nephi 3:9)
8. Also, in deception, they try to stand as sentinels for those who they perceive as having been taking advantage of or have been robbed by another group of people. They stir up a segment of the population to cry foul, to cry abuse, to cry retribution, even calling for reparations for events and situations in the past (of which they never have full and true understanding). Do you really think Giddianhi wanted to "avenge their wrongs"? This egomaniac wasn't doing anything for anyone else. It was shallow platitudes. (3 Nephi 3:10)

One author summarized this letter thus: "The epistle from Giddianhi to Lachoneus began with flattering words dripping with hypocrisy as well as an undercutting snideness."[7]

Fortunately, there are some in our day like Lachoneus and Gidgiddoni—men who are rational and humble. Consider Mormon's narrative and insights of men and leaders that had to confront or navigate men like Giddianhi. Will we see such leaders and situations in our day as the buildup to Zion occurs?

1. They were astonished at the boldness and demands (the arrogancy of those craving power). The use of the word *astonished* in this context is being surprised and amazed, not fearful. Lachoneus "could not be frightened." This astonishment is prevalent today as most people observe the

---

7. Dennis L. Largey, *Book of Mormon Reference Companion*, 250. "Elements of Giddianhi's letter echo the character, strategy, and designs of Satan." See page 292.

madness of those desperately trying to obtain positions of power and change the laws of the land. (3 Nephi 3:11–12)

2. The Lord will place just men in place that do not fear threatening words and actions from those against Him. (3 Nephi 3:12)
3. These just men will invite and inspire individuals and families to call upon "the Lord for strength" to stand when their enemies threaten their person, property, and livelihood. (3 Nephi 3:12)
4. They will call for a literal gathering. They will invite the righteous to gather unto places of refuge. People will come with families, with their substance, and resources needed for sustainability. (3 Nephi 3:13)
5. They call upon people to build mighty fortifications to withstand enemy blows. They put their energy in defending, not destroying. (3 Nephi 3:14)
6. Men like unto Lachoneus call upon all to repent of their iniquities and their rebellions. They call upon people to pray and seek deliverance from the Lord. They will be full of prophecies and words acceptable to and given by Jesus Christ. They preach the word and allow all people to choose for themselves. They do not force or manipulate. (3 Nephi 3:16)
7. They appoint those who are one with Jesus Christ to lead and direct the people. These leaders have the spirit of revelation and prophecy. They have a witness of the reality of Jesus Christ. (3 Nephi 3:18–19)
8. They act in unity and do not hesitate to correct the voice of the people when they are wrong or misguided. (3 Nephi 3:21)

A great many people hearkened unto Lachoneus and Gidgiddoni. "They did fortify themselves against their enemies; and they did dwell in one land, and in one body."[8] In this case, the Nephites

8. 3 Nephi 3:25.

and Lamanites had "deserted" their lands and took their resources and substance with them. This left certain cities "desolate." A bad plight for robbers who operated on plundering. The Nephites and Lamanites had the ability to subsist in the center of the land for seven years.[9]

Lachoneus still had to prepare for war, with all its substance and weapons. Yet he yielded to a higher spirit. Like unto Captain Moroni he was not bloodthirsty.

> Here we see a remarkable principle at work. God had commanded the Nephites as a people to fight only defensively, to go to war only as it was necessary to the preservation of their lives, their agency, their families, and their worship. . . . Christians enter war; they do not begin it. Even when it came to taking the initiative in what would appear to be a noble cause- to go into the mountains and root out the secret combinations- the sensitive Gidgiddoni declined the suggestion and explained that if they did that his people would not enjoy the approbation and thus the strength of the Lord.[10]

Lachoneus called upon Gidgiddoni for his help. Gidgiddoni had the spirit of revelation and prophecy. Religious men of great faith were usually interconnected into Nephite military operations. Perhaps we can expect some earthly leaders and government leaders of the last days to call upon men and women who have the spirit of revelation and prophecy in troubling times of war and conflict, in times of uncertainty and unrest.[11] Furthermore, what will unfold at the center place of Zion, in the center of the land, will draw not only their curiosity, but also their help and resources.

We don't know for sure, but those who united in the center of the land at this time in Nephite history seem to have been people of

---

9. 3 Nephi 4:1–4.
10. Joseph Fielding McConkie, Robert Millet, and Brent L. Top. *Doctrinal Commentary on the Book of Mormon*, vol. 4:16.
11. 3 Nephi 3:19.

> "And the land which was appointed was the land of Zarahemla, and the land which was between the land of Zarahemla and the land Bountiful, yea, to the line which was between the land Bountiful and the land Desolation" (3 Nephi 3:23).

many different persuasions and beliefs. They were called Nephites, most likely because of their civic beliefs. Not all of them were of the Church of God. The seven-year ordeal did influence their belief in the prophetic word. Mormon said that none of the Nephites doubted the words of the prophets.[12] Zion will produce such an effect. But it will take some time to get there.

I ask again, as we considered Zion, the New Jerusalem, in the center of the land, are there any relevant lessons from 3 Nephi 3 (we should probably consider chapters 2–7 in their entirety)? Some authors have asked it this way: "This passage reminds us of Enoch's city, whose gathered people 'were of one heart and one mind, and dwelt in righteousness.' In what ways might these events forecast the last days when the Saints establish a 'land of peace, a city of refuge, a place of safety for the Saints of the Most High god?'"[13]

Elder D. Todd Christofferson similarly asked: "What are the fundamentals that sustain a flourishing society, one that promotes happiness, progress, peace, and well-being among its members? We have scriptural record of at least two such thriving societies. What can we learn from them?"[14]

There is strength in numbers and in combining resources. There is strength in putting away the sword. In this Nephite conflict anyone not aligning with the robbers' efforts of plunder and murder had to choose to gather in a center place of security. The same warning has been set forth in our day. "Every man that will not take his

---

12. 3 Nephi 5:1.
13. Thomas R. Valletta, ed. *The Book of Mormon Study Guide: From Start to Finish*, 848.
14. "Sustainable Societies," *Ensign*, Nov. 2020.

sword against his neighbor must needs flee unto Zion for safety."[15] How the call comes, by proclamation or by the natural occurrences as situations and events unfold, is not known. But there will be similar gatherings of people in the future.

Additionally, there is strength in trusting in Jesus Christ. A Zion people will have plenty of experience to understand how to gain strength in troubling times. President Ezra Taft Benson once remarked that "from the Book of Mormon we learn how disciples of Christ live in times of war."[16] We can also learn how disciples of Jesus Christ lived in strength of community.

How will wars and civil unrest flooding the earth today impact the future? What brings inner peace in times of war and contention? As we recognize and develop godlike attributes of exemplary individuals in the Book of Mormon who faced war and contention in their day, we can develop the same spiritual reservoir and degree of sanctification they did. Living in mortality presents two options, two camps, in which we can enlist—the camp of the hard-hearted or the camp of the soft-hearted.[17] We can choose to stay in Babylon, or we can acquire a Zion heart and mind, which will prepare us to physically gather in unity.

We live in a day when many find themselves fighting either by choice or by the invitation of their government. It is a day when some will be separated from loved ones in conflict that has decimated their neighborhoods, communities, and nations. We may expect that many more people will have their lives interrupted and need to be relocated. War and the "sword of destruction did hang over" the people of Nephi.[18] In the coming days (and even now), we can, to some degree, expect to be in the same dilemma. How to be peaceable followers of Jesus Christ at these times will test the righteous. It will also prepare them for a Zion society.

---

15. D&C 45:68.
16. In Conference Report, October 1986, 5; or *Ensign*, November 1986, 7.
17. Alma 62:41.
18. 3 Nephi 2:19.

We are commanded to "renounce war and proclaim peace, and seek diligently to turn the hearts of the children to their fathers, and the hearts of the fathers to the children."[19] However, President Gordon B. Hinckley advocated, "There are times when we must stand up for right and decency, for freedom and civilization, just as Moroni rallied his people in his day to the defense of their wives, their children, and the cause of liberty."[20] Righteous Nephites went to war for similar reasons: "to support their lands, . . . houses, . . . wives, and their children, . . . their rights and their privileges, . . . and also their liberty, that they may worship God according to their desires."[21]

Nevertheless, Elder Robert C. Oaks, formerly of the Presidency of the Seventy and a retired military general, soberly reminded all of us, "War has a frightening ability to numb our Christian sensitivities."[22] The Lord did emphasize purchasing the land of Zion over acquiring it by blood.[23] He understands our spiritual sensitivities and how to best enlighten them rather than diminish them. We must avoid influences and behaviors that will numb our Christian sensitivities. If we don't, it will inhibit our ability to become, and gather with, a Zion people.

---

19. D&C 98:16.
20. In Conference Report, October 2001, 88; or *Ensign*, November 2001, 72.
21. See Alma 43:9; see also verses 30, 45, 47–49.
22. *Let Not Your Heart Be Troubled—A Message of Peace for Latter-day Saints in Military Service* (DVD, 2005). This 57-minute production includes remarks from Presidents Gordon B. Hinckley and Boyd K. Packer and Elders Robert C. Oaks and Lance B. Wickman.
23. See D&C 63:29–37.

10

There Is Plenty of Work Out in Front of Us

"Work is always a spiritual necessity even if, for some, work is not an economic necessity."[1]

My parents enjoyed having fun. They thoroughly enjoyed entertaining. They took us to the movies (and they left us at home and went to the movies). They frequently took us to our family's favorite restaurants. They planned and saved for vacations. They joined a bowling league. They sent us bowling (it was cheap in Las Vegas). They played cards with us and with many friends. They hosted swim parties. They took friends on drives so they could visit. Mother made chocolate chip cookies every rainy day, and everyone in the neighborhood and at school knew they were welcome to stop by to enjoy one. My father would build and provide manpower for free haunted houses at Halloween. They loved to laugh and to bring other people laughter.

But something always preceded this portion of their life: work and service.

1. Neal A. Maxwell. "Put Your Shoulder to the Wheel," *Ensign*, May 1998.

As I have aged, I have noticed the pattern and purpose of work and service more readily. Saturday morning chores always preceded play and entertainment. An individual in need was never neglected.

When I turned twelve, my father owned me. But he also owned his own plastering business. That's why he owned me. From that time on, the summers meant full-time work. He paid me six dollars an hour that first year. That wasn't bad money for a twelve-year-old in 1984. Because of the heat, work always started early, between 5:00 and 6:30 a.m. My first year of full-time summer work I was placed in a sand pile to help an older man feed a large pump that pushed plaster through a large gun hose. At the end of the hose was a nozzle man. He distributed the plaster evenly upon the wall. If that pump was running, we were placing a ninety-four-pound bag of cement into the mixer of the pump and then throwing twenty-four shovels of sand every two minutes.

As I advanced in years, I advanced in different skills and hourly wages. I began to love work, but not as much as the money. In his book *Approaching Zion*, Hugh Nibley stated, "The plan Satan proposed to Adam was to put everything in this glorious and beautiful world up for sale." He added, this has "launched a scramble that has gone on ever since Cain slew Abel, his brother, for gain."[2]

I saw this scramble firsthand in Las Vegas. Speaking of a hand, if you didn't have a good hand in cards you lost money. Not only scrambling but plundering and wasting away of money and time was right before my eyes. Gambling is an afront to work. My lack of discipline and my wallet didn't escape the madness. "Let us not confuse the ethic of work with the ethic of plunder."[3] The ethic of work is rooted in honesty, discipline, and a higher purpose.

"Zion is to be the headquarters for God's reconquest of the earth."[4] To help in this reconquest the Lord would have a people who understand work, honesty, discipline, and a higher purpose. Therefore, He strongly spoke against idleness, especially idleness in

---

2. *Approaching Zion*, 17.
3. Ibid. 11.
4. Ibid.

Zion. The Lord told foundational Saints, "The inhabitants of Zion also shall remember their labors, inasmuch as they are appointed to labor, in all faithfulness; for the idler shall be had in remembrance before the Lord."[5] Or in other words, those given to idleness will lose blessings and forfeit their inheritances in Zion.

More bluntly, the Lord said in an earlier revelation, "Thou shalt not be idle; for he that is idle shall not eat the bread nor wear the garments of the laborer."[6] Unfortunately, those initial Saints settling in Zion (Missouri) had some idlers among them. The Lord drew attention to them in this statement: "Now, I, the Lord, am not well pleased with the inhabitants of Zion, for there are idlers among them; and their children are also growing up in wickedness; they also seek not earnestly the riches of eternity, but their eyes are full of greediness."[7] The scramble to get gain, plunder, and the attitude of some to expect resources from others without effort plagued them. It plagues our day. A Zion people will eradicate this plague.

Do a search of *idle* or *idleness* in the scriptures. You will quickly discover that the Lord is blunt with the idler. We are to not idle away time, talents, our minds, and the labors of our hands. Therefore, work is a prominent principle of the gospel. Elder Neal A. Maxwell offered these thoughts: "I remind you that the gospel of work is part of 'the fulness of the gospel'. . . . Your individual mix of work will vary, understandably, by season and circumstance. . . . Knowing how to work will give you an edge in life, and experience with excellence—a special edge!"[8] School work, professional work, service, church work, part-time work, work in and around the home, and plenty of more work—it all adds up. But there is joy in work.

The New Jerusalem must be built up. This denotes work of all kinds. The Lord needs not only our hands and backs but also our

---

5. D&C 68:30.
6. D&C 42:42.
7. D&C 68:31.
8. Neal A. Maxwell. "Put Your Shoulder to the Wheel," *Ensign*, May 1998.

minds, talents, and time. It shouldn't be surprising that covenants to build up Zion accentuate these ideas.

Acquiring knowledge to use resources and muscle aptly and efficiently will require true education. The Lord has a curriculum. What are some of the secular and temporal pursuits in which we could engage to further establish the cause of Zion?

The presidents of the church sought a curriculum that would complement theology and the dissemination of our message. A practical curriculum brings practical results. Our educational endeavors should prepare us beyond the days of books and theories. Surely the Lord "comprehendeth all things, and all things are before him, and all things are round about him; and he is above all things, and in all things, and is through all things, and is round about all things; and all things are by Him, and of Him, even God, forever and ever" (see D&C 88:41). He knows what knowledge is beneficial to us, His children. He knows what subject matter should be taught and acquired and what skills and trades should be obtained for the building up of Zion. He states in the Doctrine and Covenants:

> Teach ye diligently and my grace shall attend you, that you may be instructed more perfectly in theory, in principle, in doctrine, in the law of the gospel, in all things that pertain unto the kingdom of God, that are expedient for you to understand; Of things both in heaven and in the earth, and under the earth; things which have been, things which are, things which must shortly come to pass; things which are at home, things which are abroad; the wars and the perplexities of the nations, and the judgments which are on the land; and a knowledge also of countries and of kingdoms.[9]

Consider the list of subjects that stem from the words of the Lord in this short passage of scripture. This is a list of subject matter that may be derived from these verses (I am not saying this is conclusive):

---

9. D&C 88:78–79.

1. Theory
2. Principles
3. Doctrines
4. Laws of the Gospel
5. Church Government
6. Astronomy
7. Agriculture
8. Meteorology
9. Archaeology
10. Chemistry
11. Botany
12. Geology
13. Geography
14. History
15. Current Events
16. Prophecy
17. Domestic/National Affairs
18. Foreign Affairs
19. Judgments
20. Political Structure of Nations and Kingdoms
21. Culture (Literature, Foreign Language, Arts, and so on)

There are many more subjects and disciplines that are crucial for Zion to flourish. President John Taylor proclaimed, "God expects Zion to become the praise and glory of the whole earth so that kings, hearing of her fame, will come and gaze upon her glory."[10] Knowledge and applying work will get us there. What subject matter could you study and become more familiar with? What skills and trades might help you be an equal contributor? Individually and collectively, are we meeting the Lord's expectations?

There is something to be said of manual labor and trade work. Society should not despise the working with tools or the development of professional trades. Such skills are indispensable to a

10. G. Homer Durham, *Gospel Kingdom*, 276–277.

community, especially to a Zion community. Our efforts will be of great worth in the building of the New Jerusalem. Luxury and shallow education may prove to be a difficult test in our day.

President John Taylor also urged us to "foster education and intelligence of every kind."[11] This will make us productive and creative and able to establish a Zion society. "You will see the day," President Taylor assured an audience, "that Zion will be as far ahead of the outside world in everything pertaining to learning of every kind as we are today in regard to religious matters. . . . We are, as the French would say, *en rapport*, with God; that is in communication with God. Let us live so that we can keep that up, so that angels can minister to us and the Holy Spirit dwell with us."[12]

The scriptures provide examples of those who were en rapport with God and put their efforts and mental powers to His work. Consider a few Book of Mormon examples.

Nephi set out to build a ship. His brothers said he was a fool and could not do it. But he built it, nevertheless.[13] He didn't stop there. Once off the water onto the land of their inheritance he furthered his work and industry. He taught his people to "build buildings, and to work in all manner of wood, and of iron, and of copper, and of brass, and of steel, and of gold, and of silver, and of precious ores, which were in great abundance." He built a temple. He emphasized in his record that he "did cause [his] people to be industrious, and to labor with their hands.[14]

Captain Moroni didn't just fight. He built and constructed and secured property and cities.[15] Migrating Nephites found little timber in the north, so they became experts in working with cement. They

---

11. *Journal of Discourses* 20:47–48.
12. G. Home Durham, *The Gospel Kingdom: Selections From the Writings and Discourses of John Taylor*, 275.
13. 1 Nephi 17.
14. 2 Nephi 5:15–17.
15. Alma 50.

learned a new way to build homes.[16] In the days of Nephi and Lehi there was a serious war and brutal famine. It left some cities and portions of other cities in ruin. Mormon notes that the people began to "build up their waste places."[17]

After the Savior ascended into heaven, the people "did build cities again." Some cities had been severely damaged by fire and other calamities. The Savior said a remnant of Jacob would "make the desolate cities" in the last days "to be inhabited" again.[18] This is going to take work, very enjoyable work, for those prepared and engaged in contributing their skills, trades, and mental capacities.

Brigham Young felt the Saints' efforts in the mountains were training them to build up Zion, "which consists in building houses, tabernacles, temples, streets, and every convenience and necessity to embellish and beautify . . . improving our minds in all scientific and mechanical knowledge . . . that we may know what to do with our lives and how to improve upon the facilities placed within our reach."[19]

Work and industry will be a joyful component and complement of Zion, the New Jerusalem. This may sound strange in a day of ease and entertainment, in a day when work is shunned by so many and idleness is rewarded. Some may think work and industry mean no fun, no entertainment and sport. To the contrary, I believe Zion will be full of wholesome recreational activities and sport. There will

---

16. Helaman 3.
17. Helman11:20.
18. 3 Nephi 22:3.
19. *Discourses of Brigham Young* [1954], 247. Additionally, Brigham would set forth the purpose of bringing people into a Zion community. It was a deeper meaning of Charity. "In an October 1855 epistle to the Saints, the First Presidency reminded Church members that donating to the emigrating fund helped to bring their fellow Saints to a place where they could enjoy industry and honest labor. 'This is true charity,' the presidency declared, 'not only to feed the hungry and clothe the naked, but to place them in a situation where they can produce by their own labor their subsistence'" (In *Saints, Vol. 2*, 217).

> "While we strive to be diligent in building up Zion, including our part in the gathering of the Lord's elect and the redemption of the dead, we should pause to remember that it is the Lord's work and He is doing it. He is the Lord of the vineyard, and we are His servants. He bids us labor in the vineyard with our might this 'last time,' and He labors with us. It would probably be more accurate to say He permits us to labor with Him."
>
> — D. Todd Christofferson
>
> ("Preparing for the Lord's Return," *Ensign*, May 2019)

be virtuous and uplifting entertainment. There will be relieving and relaxing fun and refreshment that will enliven the soul. But not at the expense of subduing work and creative activity. And not at the expense of promoting images and words contrary to the pure virtue of Jesus Christ.

What are we obliged to do as Saints of the last days? Wilford Woodruff succinctly laid it out. And it all denotes wonderful, joyful work: "We are obliged to build cities, town and villages, and we are obliged to gather people from every nation under heaven to the Zion of God."[20] So again, we see what is out in front of us. The sweat and blood of earlier Latter-day Saints set a fine example. I fear that example and that fire is being lost to some degree. But I am confident, unforeseen events will pull us firmly from our slumber.

There will be plenty to do. And many good people will come together in a power of work and rebuilding that has never been seen, never been equaled. This is exciting to me. Work is rewarding. Idleness is depressing. The buildup of Zion will radiate the spiritual power of work. People will take notice. It can and will influence stakes of Zion.

Several years ago, to help my boys understand work and effort as opposed to idleness and laziness, I invited them to sit on the

20. *Journal of Discourses* 16:269.

couch. I gave them each a potato. I took a picture of them as they held up their potato. The picture is now proof they were once couch potatoes. It gave us a chance to discuss how the expression "couch potato" is meant to draw attention to a lazy and inactive person, often referred to those who spend a great deal of time watching television. In all seriousness, the family discussion that night allowed us to have a genuine discussion about the principle of work and effort. In recent days President Russell M. Nelson has reminded us that "the Lord loves effort, and effort brings rewards."[21]

We will have plenty of opportunities to exert our physical and mental efforts in the coming days. This may be work in many ways we have never thought of before. There are plenty of industries that we need to be familiar with, as well as plenty of trades to acquire. There are also technology and resources still yet to be revealed. This leaves us with plenty of education and acquisition of knowledge to obtain. A Zion people will eagerly embrace all of this.

One way I can emphasize the theme of this chapter is to leave you with one more statement from Wilford Woodruff: "We can't build up Zion sitting on a hemlock slab [wood seat] singing ourselves away to everlasting bliss."[22] We can't be couch potatoes!

---

21. Joy D. Jones. "An Especially Noble Calling," *Ensign*, May 2020.
22. *Teachings of Presidents of the Church: Wilford Woodruff*, 228.

11

Consecration and Tithing—The Standing Law

"If thou obtainest more than that which would be for thy support, thou shalt give it into my storehouse."[1]

The Lord doesn't define poverty by a wage threshold. Nor does He tell us who is rich by income level. Government and civic interest groups are more than ready to declare these boundaries. And for their varied purposes they pit people against one another by the root of all evil, the love of money.[2] Who has it? Who doesn't? Who should have it? Who shouldn't? Who should have more? Who should have less? Such civic quagmire often confuses and corrupts the Lord's purposes on how to exalt all of us in a Zion society.

What the Lord desires to tell us is the condition of the heart of those rich, and those poor. Does the Lord leave out those in between, say the middle incomers? Some people are rich monetarily. Some think

1. D&C 42:55.
2. 1 Timothy 6:10.

they are rich. Others are poor. Others think they are poor and tell the whole world about it. Some don't know they are rich. All the while some don't know they are poor. Even so, many are in the middle striving for riches, living in contentment (or not), and are holding on desperately to avoid going into the realm of what the world deems poverty.

Setting all that aside, the Lord sets His teachings in context of the rich and poor, not to emphasize two groups of people on an economic strata. Clearly some have more than others and some have much less. The Lord uses such a distinction to address the condition of the heart, the attitudes, and as well as one's personal situation or place in the economic strata designated by the world.

The condition of the heart toward the cause of Zion can be cross checked by the following verses of scripture. If our hearts are not satisfied (as defined in the scriptures), we can suffocate ourselves spiritually regardless of our financial situation and worldly status. In this suffocation we inhibit our heart and mind to hear and obey truth. The Lord states it succinctly:

> And your hearts are not satisfied. And ye obey not the truth, but have pleasure in unrighteousness. Wo unto your rich men, that will not give your substance to the poor, for your riches will canker your souls; and this shall be your lamentation in the day of visitation, and of judgment, and of indignation: the harvest is past, the summer is ended, and my soul is not saved!
>
> Wo unto your poor men, whose hearts are not broken, whose spirits are not contrite, and whose bellies are not satisfied, and whose hands are not stayed from laying hold upon other men's goods, whose eyes are full of greediness, and who will not labor with your own hands![3]

Note that two verses in a row end with an exclamation point. I can't recall seeing that anywhere in the scriptures. Interestingly, I cross checked our formatted version of the Doctrine and Covenants with the Book of Commandments (1833 edition). It also has

3. D&C 56:15–17.

the exclamation points for emphasis.[4] Joseph Smith and his scribes may have been feeling a little "umph" when these words rolled onto paper. They knew the revelations they were receiving about Zion depended on the Saints' understanding, living, and correcting themselves according to this counsel. Both conditions of the rich and poor heart as described in these verses cannot stand in a Zion society. But the condition of the heart described in the verse that follows them can:

> But blessed are the poor who are pure in heart, whose hearts are broken, and whose spirits are contrite, for they shall see the kingdom of God coming in power and great glory unto their deliverance; for the fatness of the earth shall be theirs. For behold, the Lord shall come, and his recompense shall be with him, and he shall reward every man, and the poor shall rejoice. And their generations shall inherit the earth from generation to generation, forever and ever.[5]

A Zion people will individually and collectively give of their substance. A Zion people will not lay hold upon another man's goods in robbery, in greediness or in demands. A Zion people will be given to labor and not tolerate idleness. A genuine illustration of such a Zion people may be drawn from this account told by President Russell M. Nelson:

> I will never forget my first visit to West Africa in 1986. The Saints came to our meetings in great numbers. Though they had little in terms of material possessions, most came dressed in spotless white clothing. I asked the stake president how he cared for members who had so little. He replied that their bishops knew their people well. If members could afford two meals a day, no help was needed. But if they could afford only one

---

4. See https://www.josephsmithpapers.org/paper-summary/book-of-commandments-1833/136
5. D&C 56:18–20.

> meal or less—even with family help—bishops provided food, financed from fast offerings. Then he added this remarkable fact: their fast-offering contributions usually exceeded their expenses. Surplus fast offerings were then sent to people elsewhere whose needs exceeded theirs.[6]

The Lord knew that many of the Gentile nations would be favorably blessed in riches and resources. In 1831, He told a very poor group of first-generation Latter-day Saints that He would "consecrate of the riches of those who embrace my gospel among the Gentiles unto the poor of my people who are of the house of Israel."[7] Again, the rich may be those who have excess, to a small amount, or large amount. We must not forget that "according to the law every man that cometh up to Zion must lay all things before the bishop in Zion."[8] All will have something to give.

This is easy to say but not as easy to do. The warning and rebuke the Lord gave to our dear Latter-days Saints in 1834 is for us as well. A fundamental law upon which Zion is built, the law of consecration, was not observed. The Lord told them that collectively they had not learned to be obedient. As a society they had not imparted "of their substance, as becometh Saints, to the poor and afflicted." They had yet to show solid evidence of being "united according to the union required by the law of the celestial kingdom." It will be the principles of the law of the celestial kingdom that will be lived in Zion, the New Jerusalem.[9]

In 1833, Edward Partridge, the bishop in Missouri, was in a dilemma trying to understand how he was to administer the consecration of property. Joseph Smith sent him a letter to explain and encourage him in fulfilling his role as bishop. In the letter he sets forth wisdom for both the bishop and for those consecrating their property. I'll ask up front, what lessons do you draw from this letter?

---

6. "The Second Great Commandment," *Ensign*, Nov. 2019, 98.
7. D&C 42:39.
8. D&C 72:15.
9. See D&C 105:2–5. See also D&C 78:3–7; 11–19.

What do you learn about the Lord? What do you learn about the bishop? What do learn about you?

> *Sic* [Brother Edward Partridge], I proceed to answer your questions concerning the consecration of Property. First, it is not right to condescend to verry great paticulars in takeing inventories. the fact is this, that a man is bound by the law of the church to consecrate to the Bishop before he can be considered a legal heir to the Kingdom of Zion, and this too, without constraint, and unless he does this, he cannot be acknowledged before the Lord on the Church Book. Therefore, to condescend to particulars, I will tell you that every man must be his own judge how much he should receive, and how much he should suffer to remain in the hands of the Bishop. I speak of those who consecrate more than they need for the support of themselves and family The matter of consecration must be done by the mutual consent of both parties— For, to give the Bishop power to say how much every man shall have and he be obliged to comply with the Bishops judgment, is giveing to the Bishop more power than a King has and upon the other hand, to let every man say how much he needs and the Bishop obliged to comply with his judgment, is to throw Zion into confusion and make a Slave of the Bishop. The fact is, there must be a balance or equalibrium of power between the bishop and the people, and thus harmony and good will may be preserved among you. Therefore, those persons consecrating property to the Bishop in Zion, and then receiveing an inheritance back, must show reasonably to the Bishop that he wants as much as he claims. but in case the two parties can<not> come to a mutual agreement, the Bishop is to have nothing to do about receiveing their consecrations and the case must be laid before a council of twelve high Priests, the Bishop not being one of the council, but he is to lay the case before them.[10]

---

10. "Letter to Church Leaders in Jackson County, Missouri, 25 June 1833," p. [2], *The Joseph Smith Papers*, accessed February 11, 2021, https://www.josephsmithpapers.org/paper-summary/letter-to-church-leaders-in-jackson-county-missouri-25-june-1833/2.

I don't know what came to your mind as your read this. But as I formatted the statement and reread this portion of the letter, Alma's words to the people of Zarahemla came to my mind. "Are ye stripped of pride? . . . Is there one among you who is not stripped of envy?[11] We begin to see the importance of a virtuous and pure heart swelling in the people who desire a consecrated life. This is a stark contrast to the practices and solutions often implemented by the governments of men.

Something needs to intervene to help us move to the Lord's way. Again, we are brought back to receiving, accepting, and living our covenants taught in temple worship. The Lord is preparing our hearts and minds. We can begin to obtain the Lord's teachings and accept consecration through His wise instruction in temple worship. We must be unflinchingly inclined to lay all things before the Lord. Making and keeping a covenant strengthens our resolve to live after the manner of the Lord's governing principles.

This will be a distinct characteristic of a Zion people.

By tithing our increase, we begin to align with the law of consecration. In the context of Doctrine and Covenants 119, typically known as the law of tithing revelation, we learn more about how consecration will take place in Zion. Steve Harper provides the context with these words: "[The] instance of the word *tithing* is the first of three (*tithing* or *tithed*) in section 119. All of them refer to the Saints' voluntary offering of surplus property. 'And after that,' the revelation says, 'those who have thus been tithed shall pay one-tenth of all their interest annually.' The revelation does not call it a lesser law to be replaced someday, but 'a standing Law unto them forever' and applicable to all Saints everywhere."[12]

There doesn't seem to be any indication that tithing will be dismissed. It is a part of that defining characteristic of a Zion people. Consecration and sacrifice have a holistic approach of giving our time,

11. Alma 5:28–29.
12. Steve Harper, *Revelations in Context*, 252.

talents, and resources. It is so much more than money or tangible items. Many today choose consecration and sacrifice in the way they minister to others and spend their time for higher purposes, while tithing may be more narrowly looked upon as financial offerings.

With this in mind, we have already been invited to do something that will be a standing law in Zion, the New Jerusalem, and her stakes of support. The front end of living the law of consecration (as presented in Doctrine and Covenants 119) is voluntarily offering up surplus property and monies. This we will have to do when asked by the Lord. This will be followed by keeping the standing law, day by day, month to month, and year by year. That standing law is tithing. Joseph Fielding Smith wasted no words to help us understand. "Those who cannot abide the law of tithing cannot partake of this law of consecration . . . and they will be deprived an inheritance when the inheritances are divided [in Zion and her stakes]."[13]

This is how we will help, support, and encourage one another. This is how we will give those honest in heart, those eager to labor, the those virtuous in mind to contribute and create, a chance to flourish individually, in families and in Zion. In a short concise parable the Lord declared: "For what man among you having twelve sons, and is no respecter of them, and they serve him obediently, and he saith unto the one: Be thou clothed in robes and sit thou here; and to the other: Be thou clothed in rags and sit thou here - and looketh upon his sons and saith I am just? . . . I say unto you, be one; and if ye are not one ye are not mine."[14]

The Lord can and will give us further instruction and counsel regarding His law of consecration. As we are called upon to live in a more united order and lay all surplus before the Lord the details of how it works may be further clarified beyond what our current revelations declare. Joseph's letter to Edward Partridge quoted earlier in this chapter is introductory principles of how it will be administered.

---

13. *Church History and Modern Revelation*, 1:170.
14. D&C 38:26–27. See also D&C 42:30.

Until further clarifications and implementation are set forth, it may be helpful to remember that in Enoch's Zion, "there was no poor among them."[15] The Nephites' Zion generation also eliminated the gulf of the rich and poor, the bond and free.[16] New Testament Saints (at least in the Jerusalem Church) strove to have "all things common" insomuch that no one "lacked" temporally because the people consecrated their resources and allowed the apostles and the seventy to make distribution according to need.[17]

Satan tries to mimic this but for entirely different reasons—control and bondage. His desire is to rob people not only of accountability but also of purpose. He wants people to stay idle, stale, and unproductive. He finds satisfaction in reducing people to drown in selfishness and the expectation to get something for nothing. Such a way is contrary to the law of the harvest.

The Lord wants all to experience a unique individual freedom that allows them to contribute to the whole.[18] In Zion, people will be given resources and property that will be sufficient for themselves and their family.[19] For certain, any "residue" [excess] will be consecrated after all of the needs and righteous wants of its members are met.[20] The scriptures confirm that this consecration willingly lived by a Zion people will allow the resources to be accumulated to build up the New Jerusalem.[21]

Consecration, as defined by the Lord, has a brutal contrast in results than man's efforts and government programs. "You will . . . see," Elder Maxwell quipped, "that the living of one protective principle

---

15. Moses 7:18.
16. 4 Nephi 1:3.
17. Acts 4:32–35.
18. "The Lord's revelations on consecration emphasized the doctrines of individual agency, stewardship, and accountability" (Steve Harper, *Revelations in Context*, 250).
19. D&C 42:32.
20. D&C 42:33.
21. D&C 42:35; 119:2.

of the gospel is better than a thousand compensatory governmental programs—which programs are, so often, like 'straightening deck chairs on the Titanic.'"[22] Those who consecrate provide to each other: opportunity, work, individual and family growth, creativity, purpose, expansion, fulfillment, with a host of other descriptive blessings. Consecrating our all is a protective principle and will yield great results for us, our families, and others.

The synoptic gospels all have inserted in their account the story of the rich man asking the Savior what he must do to inherit eternal life. The Savior's concise yet sincere response may just be the best description of what it means for someone to consecrate. "Sell all that thou hast and distribute unto the poor . . . and come, follow me."[23] Or in restoration scripture we hear Him say: "If thou obtainest more than that which would be for thy support, thou shalt give it into my storehouse."[24]

Consecration isn't merely giving over resources or money. "It is to sanctify or make sacred or holy," Steven Harper teaches. "Possessions, time, and spiritual gifts can be made sacred by offering them, but philanthropy is not consecration, nor is making a token offering of one's abundance. . . . Consecration is keeping the two great commandments, where the key words are *love* and *all*."[25] There is a spiritual, personal component in consecration. It is becoming, not just giving.

In consecration we freely acknowledge our increases and our excesses, whether they be acquired talents and available time, or property and money. We trust the Lord's distribution method will be fulfilled in His righteousness. We come unto Him. We follow Him. We hearken to His voice and sustain His standards and commandments. The result will be holy people gathered in a holy city.

---

22. "Why Not Now?" October 1974 general conference.
23. Luke 18:18–24. See also Matthew 19:16–23 and Mark 10:17–23.
24. D&C 42:55.
25. "All Things Are the Lord's: The Law of Consecration in the Doctrine and Covenants," 215. In *Doctrine and Covenants Revelations in Context: The 37th Annual Sidney B. Sperry Symposium*, 2008.

12

Physical Environment of the City of Zion

"There is indeed an alliance between physical cleanliness and spiritual cleanliness, just as the clean body, clean home, and clean surroundings stay the spread of disease, so the clean mind, clean thoughts and acts stay the spread of evil."[1]

Again, the topic in this chapter is the antithesis of a trend that can currently be observed in our own situations and cities. All things unto our Father in Heaven and Jesus Christ are spiritual.[2] Just as the "care and cleaning of a house has eternal significance," so does the care and cleaning of a community and city. Modern cities today have a proclivity to shape inhabitants. Cities can shape an individual, families, and a people. Zion will powerfully influence her inhabitants. The physical standard of order and cleanliness will influence righteousness.[3]

---

1. John H. Vandenberg, "To Cleanse Our Souls," *Ensign*, Nov. 1975.
2. D&C 29:34.
3. See Sister Daryl V. Hoole, "Creating Clean Environment Helps Invite the Spirit," *Church News*, January 22, 1994.

Zion will set forth "perfection of beauty" as never seen in our generation (dispensation).[4] Holiness, order, and cleanliness are not just a spiritual ideal. They are physical ideals. "Cleanliness, neatness and order do not guarantee happiness, but happiness is almost impossible amidst dirt, disorder, and confusion."[5] Filthiness doesn't produce pleasantness. Nor does it produce love and peace. It often results in contention.

This will have to be understood by a people called upon to build and live in Zion. They must know how to manage themselves, their homes, and their communities to be fit candidates for Zion, the New and Holy Jerusalem. The Lord has given the instruction, "Let all things be done in cleanliness before me."[6] We marvel at the standard of cleanliness in our temples and chapels, yet seemingly forget the pattern and standard when we get home and dwell in and among our own property.

I am not talking about our homes having the same quality of structure as temples and chapels. I am talking about the way in which we maintain that with which the Lord has blessed us. Simple properties and modest homes, along with elaborate and high-quality material homes, must follow the same principle. All things and all places must be kept in cleanliness before the Lord. Perhaps this is not a comfortable subject for many. But this must be addressed. We are going for the perfection of beauty.

Think about how you feel when you enter the temples or walk onto church grounds. The buildings and grounds are beautiful, well kept, and yes, in order. The Church is the perfect example. Wherever you live or whoever you are in this Church, from dirt floors to exotic marble front entries, the issue is the same. What we are talking about is not the differences in property; it is about how we take care of that property. It is the principles of order and cleanliness. The Lord says it

---

4. Psalm 50:2.
5. See Daryl V. Hoole, "Creating Clean Environment Helps Invite the Spirit," *Church News,* January 22, 1994.
6. D&C 42:41.

simply another way: "Set in order your houses; keep slothfulness and uncleanness far from you."[7]

When I was a young parent, I used the example of the Church when my children would leave unnecessary messes (it didn't always work). In discussing this issue with students over the years a handful will always say, "Yeah, but the temple is different." I argue that it is not. Yes, temples have better carpet, better paint, nicer light fixtures, higher quality furniture, and so on, but that is not the topic at hand. The temples and ward house are void of clutter; they are simple and most definitely in order. A pattern we should follow. A pattern the city of Zion will follow.

After Edward Partridge and Sidney Rigdon heard the mission of the restored gospel in Ohio, they set off for New York. Sidney was baptized in Ohio before leaving. Edward was reluctant. He preferred to first meet the Prophet Joseph Smith. When they arrived near Palmyra, they learned that the Smiths had recently moved to Fayette, New York, twenty-six more miles to the east. Edward felt inclined to visit the Smith farm in the Manchester/Palmyra area that they had just vacated.

Could the property reveal something? From the book *Saints* we learn that "Edward wanted to look over the property, thinking the Smiths' handiwork might reveal something about their character. He and Sidney saw their well-kept orchards, their homes and outbuildings, and the low stone walls they had constructed. Each testified of the family's order and industry."[8] After this visit and witness of the family's order of living, the two men walked the rest of the day to get to the Smith home to the east. A meeting was already in progress. Sidney and Edward were able to get into the house and hear Joseph Smith for the first time.

Upon finishing his sermon, Joseph Smith asked if any in the congregation wanted to express themselves. Edward stood and

---

7. D&C 90:18.
8. *Saints*, Vol. 1 (The Standard Truth), 106–107.

conveyed "what he had seen and felt on his trip." He then presented himself for baptism, requesting Joseph to do it.[9]

Obviously, there were more details in the experience of Edward Partridge's trip that we do not have. But why would he judge so much of their character based on the order and industry of their farm? Is this a unique indicator of the nature of someone or some family? Edward had surely heard about the Smith family through gossip and circulating stories in the papers, much of which was negative or ridiculing. Edward felt something. He saw something. And it was contrary to the rumors.[10] Was he seeing a principle of Zion and a Zion people? Work and industry were laid out in the previous chapter. The Smiths had that. Additionally, their order and cleanliness taught Edward something about their nature and characters individually and as a family.

Does order and cleanliness help refine our natures and bring us into closer proximity of God? The term "cleanliness is next to godliness" isn't scripture, but it resembles the power of scripture language. As far as I can find, the statement seems to come from a sermon by religious reformer John Wesley (1703–1791).

A religious leader from our day, while contemplating "cleanliness is next to godliness," offered this thought and connection to our Hebrew fathers: "There is indeed an alliance between physical cleanliness and spiritual cleanliness, just as the clean body, clean home, and clean surroundings stay the spread of disease, so the clean mind, clean thoughts and acts stay the spread of evil. A progressive statement from the Hebrew Fathers reads, 'The doctrines of religion are resolved into carefulness, carefulness into vigorousness; vigorousness into guiltlessness; guiltlessness into [moderation]; [moderation] into cleanliness; cleanliness into godliness.'"[11]

It may be that Wesley pulled his phrase from the Hebrew fathers. Note how cleanliness is part of a lifestyle, a gospel living

9. Ibid.
10. See Joseph Smith—History 1:61.
11. As quoted in Elder John H. Vandenberg, "To Cleanse Our Souls," *Ensign*, Nov. 1975.

that influences progression to godliness. The building of Zion is a step closer to having Jesus Christ dwell among us. For these reasons, Isaiah's words will be fulfilled, standing in contrast with what we will witness in modern cities. The city of Zion will be "sought out, A city not forsaken."[12]

As he continued to teach temporal salvation and points of improvement for arriving Saints in the Salt Lake Valley, Brigham Young summarized the matter thus: "We will have a city clean and in order."[13] Often, visitors would positively remark on this cleanliness and order. Remember, this was going to be an exemplary stake of Zion. And it wasn't just about cleanliness and order but about reclaiming and preparing for something better. Brigham Young counseled:

> Brethren and sisters, I wish you to continue in your ways of welldoing. . . . Shall we not strive to prepare ourselves as much as possible for the coming of the Son of Man? . . . This earth must become a paradise—must be purged of the sin that has been upon it for many generations, for all sin and iniquity must be swept from it, and a people be prepared for the coming of the Son of Man. . . . The Saints will increase, the Spirit of wisdom and knowledge will increase, and every grace of the Spirit of the Lord Jesus Christ must increase upon the earth, until a people and place are so prepared that the Saviour can come and finish the work given him to do, when he will present the kingdom to the Father. There is a great work for the Saints to do. Progress, and improve upon, and make beautiful everything around you. Cultivate the earth and cultivate your minds. Build cities, adorn your habitations, make gardens, orchards, and vineyards,

12. Isaiah 62:12.
13. This quotation and the several thoughts coming in the next few paragraphs were influenced by Craig D. Galli's article: "Building Zion: The Latter-day Saint Legacy of Urban Planning." I highly recommend an entire read of this article if you want to understand the physical environment of Zion communities [see *BYU Studies Quarterly*, 44:1, 2005].

> and render the earth so pleasant that when you look upon your labours you may do so with pleasure, and that angels may delight to come and visit your beautiful locations.[14]

A few years later he would come back to this theme. "We are trying to be the image of those who live in heaven; we are trying to pattern after them, to look like them, to walk and talk like them, to deal like them, and build up the kingdom of heaven as they have done. I think that after awhile we shall attain to the very image and likeness of the children of God who have lived before us."[15] How do we make beautiful everything around us? How do we continue to obtain this order and cleanliness, this reclaiming and preparing for the Savior? George A. Smith (who lived in Brigham Young's day) offered some practical advice:

> Incorrect traditions, though long followed, have to be surrendered, and we have to build up Zion. The plan of Zion contemplates that the earth, the gardens, and fields of Zion, be beautiful and cultivated in the best possible manner. Our traditions have got to yield to that plan, circumstances will bring us to that point, and eventually we shall be under the necessity of learning and adopting the plan of beautifying and cultivating every foot of the soil of Zion in the best possible manner. When the Saints become instructed, when this people become united as they should be, when they learn things as they should learn them, they will not be subject to the constant and unpleasant annoyances to which they have been subject. . . . If I understand the order of building up the kingdom, it is a spiritual work, on every occasion, to give proper instructions necessary for the good of the kingdom. Very small matters lead sometimes to great results. . . . You must see that some temporal arrangements are necessary, to enable men to enjoy that quiet which would be desirable in attempting to worship our Heavenly Father.[16]

14. Brigham Young, in *Journal of Discourses*, 8:83–84, June 12, 1860.
15. Brigham Young, in *Journal of Discourses*, 9:170, January 26, 1862.
16. George A. Smith, in *Journal of Discourses*, 3:282–283, April 6, 1856.

The physical environment of Zion must be addressed, George Albert Smith argued. As we set temporal arrangements in order, we are better able to "enjoy the quiet." I believe the context of his words lends itself to revelation and joy. As we put forth our efforts in Zion, the Lord will bless us with joy and revelation. We can't get there if we don't have a stillness or "quiet" to worship. Our surroundings and our temporal situations, if not in order, can constantly distract and derail us from such moments. I believe Zion is set apart by the work and order set forth in its boundaries but also set apart by the fruit of joy and revelation.

Many have observed the plat image sent from the Prophet Joseph Smith to the Saints in Missouri (see below). Though undiscernible at first glance, this image represents design and distinction that would be paramount in Zion communities. It was approved by the prophet Joseph Smith as a draft to Edward Partridge and other local leaders in Missouri. This City of Zion plat was intended to

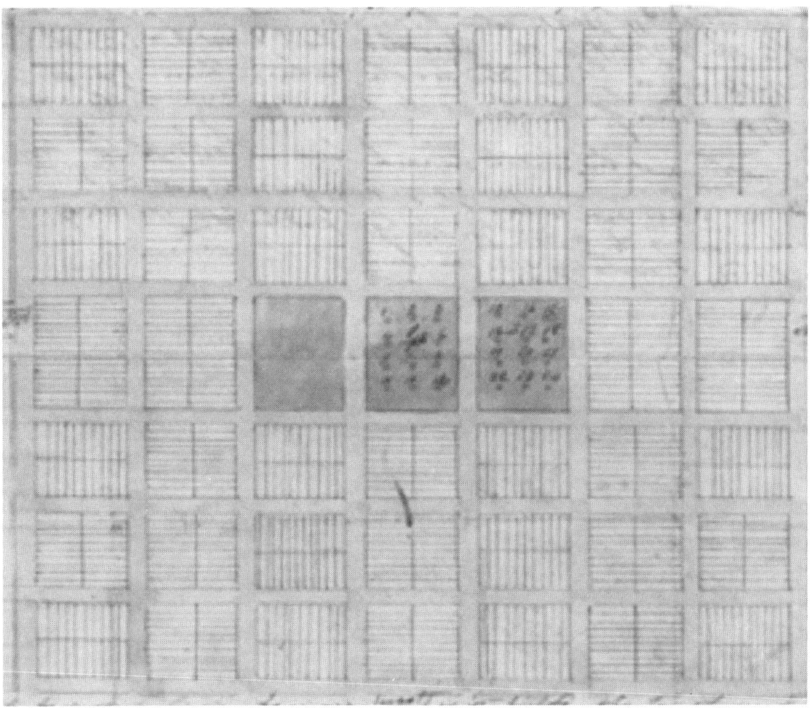

describe structures and standards for a city of one-square-mile.[17] This plat gave attention to a city center with essential buildings (temples) dealing with temporal and spiritual salvation. Half-acre lots were set aside for residential homes. Joseph Smith's initial descriptions gave these details. One author has summarized:

> The four major streets had 132-foot widths, other streets had 82.5-foot widths, and all were oriented to the cardinal directions. Houses, normally to be built of brick or stone, would be set back twenty-five feet from the streets with gardens and orchards for beauty and sustenance. The Prophet Joseph intended that residents locate their barns and stables at the community's edge, surrounded by agricultural lands and open space. The density of the community when fully populated would be relatively high for a frontier town—eight people per lot. After achieving a population of between fifteen and twenty thousand inhabitants, growth into the immediately adjacent surrounding area would not be allowed. Rather, a new satellite community would be settled beyond a buffer or greenbelt between the new and old communities.
>
> Margin notes reveal Joseph Smith's intentions to maintain a compact urban design: 'When the square is thus laid off and supplied, lay off another in the same way, and so fill up the world in the last days.' Joseph intended that all members of the community live within the city: 'Let every man live in the city, for this is the city of Zion.' Farmers would live side by side with merchants and professionals, rather than on the outskirts of the community or on remote ranches and farms.[18]

I will not continue to give all the particulars and context of the plat. Many people have written and spoken extensively about this. I will leave you with this final point about order and cleanliness. This plat shows that there were designs and ideas the Lord felt to give Latter-day Saints of the 1830s who were going to establish the foundation of Zion.

---

17. See *Saints*, Vol. 1:169–170.
18. Craig D. Galli, "Building Zion: The Latter-day Saint Legacy of Urban Planning," *BYU Studies Quarterly*, 44:1, 2005, see pages 113–114.

Brigham Young and others who followed him "adapted this City of Zion Plat for us in settling" communities in the western regions of the United States.[19] Likewise, we can expect that future city plats will be set forth as modern situations regarding resources, technology, homes, infrastructure, and even changes to topography are brought into consideration. Some details from the original details provided by Joseph Smith in the 1830s may be concrete across time and others could be strikingly different.

One thing is certain. The house of the Lord—temples—and all the temporal buildings that will flank its purpose will be part of the physical environment of Zion. They will reflect the purposes and work of Jesus Christ He promised His Saints. The physical environment of the roads, homes, and yards will reflect Jesus Christ, His creations and His creative power, and His holiness.

If I were to try and summarize work, industry (see chapter 10), and order and cleanliness (this chapter) in one word, I would use the world *holiness*. Elder D. Todd Christofferson expressed: "If we yearn to dwell in Christ and have Him dwell in us, then holiness is what we seek, in both body and spirit. We seek it in the temple, whereon is inscribed 'Holiness to the Lord.' We seek it in our marriages, families, and homes. We seek it each week as we delight in the Lord's holy day. We seek it even in the details of daily living: our speech, our dress, our thoughts."[20] Such seeking and living after the manner of holiness will impact most remarkably the physical environment of Zion.

That yearning to dwell with Christ will move a people to gather and build Zion, the New Jerusalem. Saints and others will dispose of that which is not needed. They will drop incorrect traditions and practices that don't align with the pattern and standards. They will gladly adopt and go to work being governed by the revealed word of Jesus Christ.

---

19. Ibid.
20. "The Living Bread Which Came Down from Heaven," *Ensign*, Nov. 2017.

13

Gathering to Zion in Families

"We as a people will become more united amid increasing conflict. We will be gathered in the spiritual strength of groups and families filled with gospel light."[1]

All canonized scriptural accounts begin in the context of families. The Old Testament gives us Adam and Eve being placed in the garden and commanded to multiply and replenish the earth, followed by the account of Father Abraham's family. The New Testament sets forth the births of Jesus Christ and John the Baptist in a families. The Book of Mormon gives us Lehi's family leaving Jerusalem with Ishmael's family. The Doctrine and Covenants is unique because it has its beginnings with strong families in historical context flanking the early revelations—the Smiths, the Knights, and the Whitmers, to name a few.

Unfortunately, we don't have ancient records that give details as to the order of priesthood in the days of the patriarchs (Patriarchal Priesthood). However a simple truth stated in the Pearl of Great Price declares the "same Priesthood, which was in the beginning,

1. President Henry B. Eyring. "Prayers of Faith," *Ensign*, May 2020, 28.

shall be in the end of the world also."[2] When this is to be, we don't know. But all indications are that it will be the antithesis of the patterns and behaviors of the world regarding family, human relationships, and associations.

The strength of family will be an integral part of Zion.

Most people see firsthand the condition and state of the family today. In many cases it is terribly saddening, and in other cases it is brutally maddening. Nonetheless, it will be families who will be called upon to gather to Zion. As early as March 1831 the Lord began emphasizing that after the place was designated for the City of Zion and land purchased "then shall ye begin to be gathered in *with your families, every man according to his family,* according to his circumstances, and as is appointed by the presidency and the bishop of the Church." This is the first reference to *families* gathering to Zion. The Lord said He would provide further revelation on the matter.[3]

Four months later the Lord gave the second reference to Zion being established by families. He reminded Joseph Smith that those called upon to lay the foundation in Zion were to do so with their families. "And thus let those of whom I have spoken be planted in the land of Zion, as speedily as can be, *with their families,* to do those things even as I have spoken. And now concerning the gathering—let the bishop and the agent make preparations *for those families* which have been commanded to come to this land, as soon as possible, and plant them in their inheritance."[4]

In both revelations the Lord designates the importance of the bishop and the presidency (or agent). It seems that today this would be in reference to the First Presidency, the Quorum of the Twelve Apostles, and the Presiding Bishopric (or those they designate). They have keys to declare and offer the inheritances of Zion according to families. Zion will be a city of order. Strong families will complement this order.

2. Moses 6:7.
3. D&C 48:6; emphasis added.
4. D&C 57:14–15; emphasis added.

In the April 2021 general conference, we learned that "more than half of adults in the Church today are widowed, divorced, or not yet married."[5] This current situation of Church membership doesn't negate the Lord's teachings on families being sent to Zion. Nor does being widowed, divorced, or not yet married disqualify someone from receiving an inheritance in Zion. Regardless of our status, the faithful who desire to make and keep covenants will be organized according to family. Organization in Zion seems to be centered in family rather than any other type of institution.

In today's environment the connotation of a patriarch is very negative. This is not surprising because the term "has come to be associated with male domination, chauvinism, sexism, and discrimination. Indeed, we should not expect that something so very important in the great plan of happiness as the patriarchal order should come forth without opposition, whether in terms of abuse, distortion, or misunderstanding."[6] In my opinion many in the world have "despised the words of plainness" on this subject. We have "sought for things that [we] could not understand." We have "looked beyond the mark."[7]

To bring up patriarchal order in today's environment can bring annoyance and wrath. Maybe this is one reason the Lord has given little information or accounts regarding the days of the patriarchs. I can't imagine how in today's world, principles of the patriarchs' days would be misconstrued, perverted, mocked, and indeed abused. Therefore, because the Lord has revealed very little to this point, it is best to state what we do know. I will only provide a few thoughts for you to consider in conjunction with family order in Zion the New Jerusalem.

As noted at the beginning of this chapter, man and woman in marriage and children—sons, and daughters—are expressly mentioned throughout scripture. Family is the setting of celestial glory.

---

5. M. Russell Ballard, "Hope in Christ," April 2021 general conference. See also Gerrit W. Gong, "Room in the Inn," April 2021 general conference.
6. Robert Millet, *Selected Writing of Robert L. Millet: Gospel Scholars Series*, 277.
7. Jacob 4:14.

President Russell M. Nelson has a unique way to express divine truth succinctly: "In God's eternal plan, salvation is an individual matter; exaltation is a family matter."[8] Everything about Zion will be with exaltation in mind. It will build up to and pattern a heavenly society. A pattern after the order of families.

The patriarchal order is within the operating powers of the Melchizedek Priesthood. According to Robert Millett, "It is, in fact, the new and everlasting covenant of marriage, an order entered into by men and women whenever they are married in the temple by one having proper sealing authority. . . . An order of family government where a man and woman enter into a covenant with God—just as did Adam and Eve—to be sealed for eternity, to have posterity, and to do the will and work of God throughout their mortality."[9]

The patriarchal order had a unique autonomy associated with it. "From evidence given in the Book of Abraham the divine patriarchal order that existed before the flood held political, as well as ecclesiastic, jurisdiction in the earth. Within this divine family order such righteous figures as Adam and Noah reigned as kings over the earth, as well as functioning as prophets, priests, and patriarchs within the divine order."[10] Additionally, "as a significant part of the restoration of all things in the latter days, the divine patriarchal order is to be re-established upon the earth before the Lord comes in His glory."[11] Consider this autonomy in governing with the idea of Zion having its own sovereignty. "The patriarchal order of the priesthood is the organizing power and principle of celestial family life. It is the ultimate and ideal form of government."[12]

---

8. "Salvation and Exaltation," *Ensign*, May, 2008, 10.
9. Millet , 277–279.
10. Hyrum L. Andrus. *Doctrinal Commentary on the Pearl of Great Price*, 365.
11. Ibid. 383.
12. Lynn A. McKinlay. "Patriarchal Order of the Priesthood." In *Encyclopedia of Mormonism*, 3:1067

Zion will have a higher order of government. It will be sustained by righteous families. A righteous father and mother will be significant pillars.[13] They will be united in the affairs and will of Jesus Christ. Such men and women who are united as parents play vital roles in blessing a Zion society. Six weeks before his martyrdom, Joseph Smith publicly declared: "I advise all to go on to perfection, and search deeper and deeper into the mysteries of godliness. A man [and woman] can do nothing for [themselves] unless God direct [them] in the right way; and the priesthood is for that purpose."[14]

The patriarchal priesthood, this same priesthood that was in the beginning of the world and will be prevalent at the end of the world, is an eternal family order. Hence, the importance of a house of the Lord being established in the city of Zion and her stakes. Though world trends try to disguise it or dismiss it, there are happy marriages between men and women. There are married couples who are being directed in the right way. God our Father, Jesus Christ, and the Holy Ghost are influencing them.

To sustain a Zion society by the family, the Lord will have to pluck people out from cities and families in their varied situations. There will be those who want the structure and blessings of marriage and family. Part of the gathering is to find them. Jehovah told Jeremiah that He would "take one of a city, and two of a family, and I will bring [them] to Zion."[15] He also told Jeremiah

---

13. In November of 2020 President Eyring reiterated the role of sisters, daughters, granddaughters, and the women they "have nurtured will be at the heart of creating that society of people who will join in glorious association with the Savior. You will be an essential force in the gathering of Israel and the creation of a Zion people who will dwell in peace in the New Jerusalem." (See "Sisters in Zion," *Ensign*, Nov. 2020).
14. "History, 1838–1856, volume F-1 [1 May 1844–8 August 1844]," *The Joseph Smith Papers*, 16, accessed February 5, 2021, https://www.josephsmithpapers.org/paper-summary/history-1838-1856-volume-f-1-1-may-1844-8-august-1844/22.
15. Jeremiah 3:14.

that He would "be the God of all the families of Israel, and they shall be my people."[16]

In our day, the Savior comforted those Saints who were driven out of western Missouri by stating: "Zion shall not be moved out her place, *notwithstanding her children are scattered.* They that remain, and are pure in heart, shall return, and come to their inheritances, *they and their children*, with songs of everlasting joy, to build up the waste places of Zion."[17]

Such marriages, families, and governance by righteous men and women will be magnified and expanded in Zion, the New Jerusalem. The Lord will gather His children to Zion accordingly, as He declared, *according to* and *with their families.*

16. Jeremiah 31:1.
17. D&C 101:17–18; emphasis added.

14

Joseph Smith Is Not Dead

"I see it, and it will be so."[1]

Elder Neal A. Maxwell succinctly stated, "Death is a mere comma, not an exclamation point!"[2] Joseph Smith (as with all who have laid the mortal body aside) is not dead, just in another realm of existence. He is still a prophet, a seer, and now a messenger with greater territory. "There are two kinds of beings in heaven," he said before his death. "Angels, who are resurrected personages, having bodies of flesh and bones" and "spirits of just men made perfect, they who are not resurrected, but inherit the same glory."[3]

Therefore, Joseph Smith, with a host of others, can be, are, and will be messengers sent to mortality to help the work of the Jesus Christ push forward. Joseph Smith understood this before going to the world of the spirits. If righteousness and truth are going

1. *Saints*, Vol. 1, 131. See also *The Ohio Star* (Ravenna, Ohio) 2, no. 47 (24 November 1831). Available at the Digital Collections of the BYU Library.
2. "Shine As Lights in the World," *Ensign*, May 1983, 11.
3. D&C 129:1–3.

to flood the earth, there will have to be a joint venture involving many individuals. "Men and angels are to be co-workers in bringing to pass this great work" he said. And "Zion is to be prepared, even a new Jerusalem, for the elect that are to be gathered from the four quarters of the earth, and to be established an holy city, for the tabernacle of the Lord shall be with them."[4]

The Prophet Joseph Smith not only saw and understood the Zion ideal, but he also saw that many people would help bring it about. The gathering of the elect from the four corners of the earth to a holy city will require the aid from other realms of existence.[5] One of the greatest seers and servants of the Lord has not been absent or disinterested or released—so to speak. Joseph Smith is a key player in what is unfolding. "Millions shall know 'Brother Joseph' again," W.W. Phelps penned shortly after the prophet's martyrdom.[6] Perhaps it might be more accurate to say "billions." Notwithstanding, Elder Neil L. Anderson affirmed, "In our society beyond the veil of death, we will clearly understand the sacred calling and divine mission of the Prophet Joseph Smith."[7]

The scriptures and statements from Joseph's contemporaries give us further insight into that sacred calling and divine mission. It's not over. Ancient prophets saw his day. Joseph of Egypt not only saw the ministry of a great seer in the last days but declared his name to be Joseph. Lehi felt inclined to pull from the brass plates, which had Joseph of Egypt's account to teach his posterity about a great

4. "History, 1838–1856, volume B-1 [1 September 1834–2 November 1838]," *The Joseph Smith Papers*, 623, accessed February 1, 2021, https://www.josephsmithpapers.org/paper-summary/history-1838-1856-volume-b-1-1-september-1834-2-november-1838/77.
5. Moses 7:62. We know through revelation that there are unembodied spirits, those with mortal bodies, those disembodied at what we call death, and resurrected personages. It doesn't seem strange to think that all may have a part to play as co-workers of building up and gathering the elect to Zion.
6. Hymn 27, Hymns of The Church of Jesus Christ of Latter-day Saints (Salt Lake City, UT: The Church of Jesus Christ of Latter-day Saints, 1985).
7. "Joseph Smith," *Ensign*, Nov. 2014, 31.

seer that would help the Lord restore all things.[8] Joseph Smith's prophetic ministry is mentioned in the Book of Mormon.[9]

Brigham Young observed the significance of Joseph Smith's life thus:

> It was decreed in the counsels of eternity, long before the foundations of the earth were laid, that he, Joseph Smith, should be the man, in the last dispensation of this world, to bring forth the word of God to the people, and receive the fulness of the keys and power of the Priesthood of the Son of God. The Lord had his eyes upon him, and upon his father, and upon his father's father, and upon their progenitors clear back to Abraham, and from Abraham to the flood, from the flood to Enoch, and from Enoch to Adam. He has watched that family and that blood as it has circulated from its fountain to the birth of that man. He was fore-ordained in eternity to preside over this last dispensation.[10]

We should not limit Joseph's foreordination to thirty-eight years of mortal life, including a fourteen-to-seventeen-year ministry. Brigham Young didn't. He understood that Joseph would preside over the last dispensation. So did Heber C. Kimball. Let me provide you with some direct statements by these two men to help us see, understand, and feel what they knew to be true. There are plenty of other similar statements, but this will suffice.

> *Brigham Young*: "Joseph Smith, Junior, will again be on this earth dictating plans . . . and he will never cease his operations,

8. Study JST, Genesis 50:24–38 and 2 Nephi 3.
9. One subject quietly interspersed in the Book of Mormon is the prophetic calling of Joseph Smith. Many ancient prophets within the Nephite record foresaw and clearly understood his latter-day work. The following verses are possible examples: Alma 37:23; 3 Nephi 21:9–11; Mormon 8:14–16, 25; Ether 5:1–2; 2 Nephi 3:6–16, 24; 21:1; 27:6–22.
10. *Discourses of Brigham Young*, 108.

under the directions of the Son of God, until the last ones of the children of men are saved that can be, from Adam till now."[11]

"There is an almighty work to perform in the spirit world. Joseph has not yet got through there. When he finishes his mission in the spirit world, he will be resurrected, but he is not yet done there. . . . When his spirit again quickens his body, he will ascend to heaven, present his resurrected body to the Father and the Son, receive his commission as a resurrected being, and visit his brethren on this earth, as did Jesus after His resurrection."[12]

Heber C. Kimball: "I am pretty sure of one thing: we shall go to Jackson County, Missouri; that is, those who do right and honor their callings, doing what they have been told to do. You will be blessed, and you will see the day when Presidents [Brigham] Young, [Heber C.] Kimball, and [Daniel H.] Wells, and the Twelve Apostles will be in Jackson County, Missouri, laying out your inheritances. In the flesh? Of course. We should look well without being in the flesh! We shall be there in the flesh, and all our enemies cannot prevent it. 'Brother Wells, you may write that. You will be there, and Willard [Richards] will be there, and also Jedediah [M. Grant], and Joseph and Hyrum Smith, and David [W. Patten], and Parley [P. Pratt]; and the day will be when I will see those men in the general assembly of the Church of the First Born, in the great council of God in Jerusalem, too. Will we want you to be along? I heard Joseph say twice that Brother Brigham and I should be in that council in [New] Jerusalem, when there should be a uniting of the two divisions of God's government."[13]

The Doctrine and Covenants provides evidence of the continued influence and ministry of the Prophet Joseph Smith here and in

---

11. *Journal of Discourses* 7:289, October 9, 1859.
12. *Journal of Discourses* 4:285–286, March 15, 1857.
13. *Journal of Discourses* 9:27, April 7, 1861.

the world of spirits. Consider the following in connection with the buildup of Zion the New Jerusalem.

> "I, the Lord, will give unto my servant Joseph Smith, Jun., power that he shall be enabled to discern by the Spirit those who shall go up unto the land of Zion, and those of my disciples who shall tarry."[14]

> "I am the Lord thy God, and I gave unto thee, my servant Joseph, an appointment, and restore all things. Ask what ye will, and it shall be given unto you according to my word."[15]

> "Verily I say unto you [Joseph Smith], the keys of this kingdom shall never be taken from you, while thou art in the world, neither in the world to come. Nevertheless, through you shall the oracles be given to another, yea, even unto the Church."[16]

> "I am with [you], and my hand shall be over [you]; and the keys which I have given unto [you] . . . shall not be taken from [you] till I come."[17]

Doctrine and Covenants 101:43–62 contains a modern-day parable concerning the redemption of Zion. In this parable of the nobleman and the olive trees we learn of servants and church members who failed to do as the Lord directed on His choice spot of land. The Lord called upon one of His servants to help set things right and reclaim the land taken by His enemies. The servant was sent to redeem this choice piece of land. However, it was made know unto Him and the other servants that went with Him, that this

14. D&C 63:41.
15. D&C 132:40.
16. D&C 90:3–4.
17. D&C 112:15.

redemption of the land would not occur until "after many days."[18]

Two months after this parable was given the Lord declared who the servant in the parable had reference to. "My servant Joseph Smith, Jun., is the man to whom I likened the servant to whom the Lord of the vineyard spake in the parable."[19] Adding a personal request to the Saints then (and I believe to Saints today and those following us), "pray earnestly that peradventure my servant Joseph Smith Jun., may go with you, and preside in the midst of my people, and organize my kingdom upon the consecrated land, and establish the children of Zion upon the laws and commandments which have been given unto you."[20]

Joseph Smith is not dead. He has an intimate interest in the unfolding events leading up to the organization of the people of God upon the land of Zion in the holy city. He will help set forth the laws and commandments by which Zion will be governed. He is not the only one. The presiding "President of the office of the High Priesthood" will also be called upon.[21] But, Joseph Smith does have a position of authority in the dispensation of the fulness of times.

---

18. D&C 101:62.
19. D&C 103:21. Though many others suggest that D&C 103:15–20 are references to a future president of the Church, I believe they have reference to Joseph Smith. I hold that he is the "man" in verse 16 and one of the "angels" in verse 19. Note that the Lord also says "angels" will help redeem Zion, which is one of the points of this chapter. Also verse 21 as quoted in the text of this chapter declares Joseph Smith as the servant whom the Lord designated. I don't think it wise to separate these verses and take it out of the context of the revelation. Additionally, I do believe D&C 105:36 is in reference to Joseph Smith as well (this is just my opinion).
20. D&C 103:35. I personally do not believe this is only about Zion's Camp and the organization of leadership in the Church that came after Zion's Camp. I hold this statement as a broad reference to further work Joseph Smith will and has been completing.
21. D&C 107:91. "And again, the duty of the President of the office of the High Priesthood is to preside over the whole Church, and to be like unto Moses." On January 21st 1836 Joseph Smith Sr. gave his son Joseph Smith Jr. a blessing. In it he blessed him to "lead the Church as a latter-day Moses" (see *Saints* Vol. 1:233)

He and others will be sent to help organize and inspire the work of those in flesh (mortality) that will need to be accomplished.

Let's return to Brigham Young, who matter-of-factly stated: "About the time that the temples of the Lord will be built and Zion is established . . . there will be strangers in your midst, walking with you, talking with you. They will enter into your houses and eat and drink with you, go to meetings with you, and begin to open your minds, as the Savior did to the two disciples who walked out in the country in days of old [Emmaus]."[22]

Now that we are nearly 200 years removed from the days of the foundation of the Restoration, it may be helpful to remember that we still believe in angelic visitations setting in order the work of Jesus Christ. "Have angels ceased to appear unto the children of men? . . Nay."[23] Joseph Smith declared: "We are the favored people that God has made choice of to bring about the Latter Day Glory. . . . And all things whether in heaven or on earth will be in one, even in Christ. The heavenly priesthood will unite with the earthly, to bring about those great purposes. . . . The Heavenly Priesthood are not idle spectators; the Spirit of God will be showered down from above, it will dwell in our midst."[24]

This doesn't seem to be the language of someone who expected to die and go off to a quiet spot and sit in idleness and indifference. Like Joseph Smith, I do believe you and I will be even more excited and more engaged in helping Zion, the New Jerusalem, and all her stakes flourish in the world of spirits and in a future resurrected state.

---

22. *Journal of Discourses* 6:294–295, August 15, 1852.
23. Moroni 7:36–37.
24. "History, 1838–1856, volume C-1 [2 November 1838–31 July 1842]," *The Joseph Smith Papers*, 1327–1328, accessed February 5, 2021, https://www.josephsmithpapers.org/paper-summary/history-1838-1856-volume-c-1-2-november-1838-31-july-1842/501. Of note as well is the prominence of Father Adam. Everything is under his direction. In bringing attention to Joseph Smith's everlasting ministry I do not excuse Adam's presiding keys of salvation. See D&C 78:16.

15

What Was It like in 1831? What Is It like Now?

"Zion is Zion because of the character, attributes, and faithfulness of her citizens."[1]

What was the cultural and social environment like in western Missouri in 1831? The western part of the United States in 1831 was a stark contrast to what the Saints moving from the eastern United States were accustomed to. William W. Phelps, who lived in western Missouri in 1831, helps us step back in time. He provided his own personal observation in these words: "The inhabitants [western Missouri] are emigrants from Tennessee, Kentucky, Virginia, the Carolinas, and with customs, manners, modes of living and climate entirely different from the northerner and they hate Yankees worse than snakes, because they cheated them. . . . The people are proverbially idle or lazy, and most ignorant; reckoning no body equal to themselves in many respects, . . . it is a slave holding state."[2]

---

1. D. Todd Christofferson. "Come to Zion," *Ensign*, Nov. 2008.
2. *Ontario Phoenix*, September 7, 1831.

Levi Hancock, attempting to give them some credit, described the inhabitants of the region this way:

> The people we met were good livers *if there were a mind to be*, but the way they managed was more like beasts than like humans. They had dogs, horses, cows, and pigs, and chickens, in abundance around the house and in the house and mixed together. In the cold weather doors were open night and day, snow flying and wind blowing through. The cracks were not chinked. They used rags for beds, ground for floors. The children were ragged and dirty. They had corn pudding and dogger to eat, with a little bacon and sassafras tea, is the people's living here. When they have an abundance of horses, cattle, and cows they might spare and make themselves and family comfortable. Land is all they want.[3]

A few years earlier, a Reverend John Mason Peck described what he witnessed as a frontier missionary. Note he is describing about half the population in his opinion, not all. But it gives us some indicators why about thirteen years later incoming Saints had to encounter what they did.

> One half, at least, of the Anglo-American population were infidels of a low and indecent grade, and utterly worthless for any useful purposes of society. Of the class I allude to, I cannot recollect an individual who was reclaimed, or became a respectable citizen. . . . This class despised and vilified religion in every form, were vulgarly profane, even to the worst forms of blasphemy, and poured out scoffing's, and contempt on the few Christians in the village. Their nightly orgies were scenes of drunkenness and profane revelry. Among the frantic rites observed were the mock celebration of the Lord's Supper, and burning the Bible. The last ceremony consisted in raking a place in the hot coals of a wood fire, and burying therein the book of God with shouting's,

3. *The Life of Levi Hancock*, ed. Clara E. H. Lloyd, Church History Library, The Church of Jesus Christ of Latter-day Saints, 48.

> prayers, and songs. The boast was often made that the Sabbath never had crossed, and never should cross the Mississippi [River].[4]

This is a very shallow and ignorant boast. But I am sure many of those described deeply meant it and acted in a way to see it through. Joseph Smith had his own words for the people populating western Missouri in the 1830s. Many of the Saints had come from "a highly cultivated state of society" in the east. "How natural it was to observe the degradation, leanness of intellect, ferocity, and jealousy of a people that were nearly a century behind the times."[5] Years later he would revisit what those initial Saints sent to build up Zion, the center place, were up against. "As we could not associate with our neighbors (who were, many of them, of the basest of men, and had fled from the face of civilized society, to the frontier country to escape the hand of justice), in their midnight revels, their Sabbath breaking, horse racing and gambling; they commenced at first to ridicule, then to persecute."[6]

The Saints purchased lands and set up their own neighborhoods amidst these people described. The Saints weren't isolationist in a strict sense. But neither were the original settlers. They meddled and persecuted the Saints and sought to ruin their business and church affairs. Joseph's remark that they could not associate with their neighbors wasn't because they didn't want to or had lifted their nose and necks to them. The populace was at brutally opposite ends of desires and purposes.

You can't force neighborliness with people who don't want to be neighborly. And Joseph acknowledged while in Liberty Jail that the

---

4. *Forty Years of Pioneer Life: Memoir of John Mason Peck D.D.*, ed. Rufus Babcock [1864], 87.
5. *History of the Church* 1:189. See also "History, 1838–1856, volume A-1 [23 December 1805–30 August 1834]," *The Joseph Smith Papers*, 127, accessed December 22, 2020, https://www.josephsmithpapers.org/paper-summary/history-1838-1856-volume-a-1-23-december-1805-30-august-1834/133.
6. "History, 1838–1856, volume E-1 [1 July 1843–30 April 1844] [addenda]," *The Joseph Smith Papers*, 9 [addenda], accessed March 24, 2021, https://www.josephsmithpapers.org/paper-summary/history-1838-1856-volume-e-1-1-july-1843-30-april-1844/432 .

Saints at times weren't always the best neighbors and most dignified members of the Church. Before the first decade of the Church ended he would write: "How vain and trifling have been our spirits, our conferences, our councils, our meetings, our private as well as public conversations—too low, too mean, too vulgar, too condescending for the dignified characters of the called and chosen of God."[7]

For multiple reasons, the cultural environment was very difficult. It would take years to change this cultural or social environment. The "friction between Latter-day Saints and local settlers was complicated." Major points that caused that friction could be competition for cheap land; opposite views on the slavery issue; how to treat Indians; political influence and power; economic approach within and without the groups; religion itself and the belief in modern revelation; Latter-day Saint attitudes about building Zion in exclusiveness; and the nature of a frontier. In short, all kinds of characters lived in Missouri. Some were there to hide from the law, and others were trying to establish God's law.[8] Friction may be a light term as these conditions are understood in their day.

Joseph Smith believed that the lack of sociability and civility, along with the "privations and inconveniences" (in 1831), could be overcome by the "hand of industry, the refinement of society, and the polish of science."[9] And of course he spent his remaining years teaching and setting forth the ordinances and covenants of

---

7. "History, 1838–1856, volume C-1 [2 November 1838–31 July 1842][b]," *The Joseph Smith Papers*, 904[b], accessed December 22, 2020, https://www.josephsmithpapers.org/paper-summary/history-1838-1856-volume-c-1-2-november-1838-31-july-1842/86.
8. Midwest Church History Participant Guide, 2008. Many of the citations above are a gathering of sources in this guidebook. I was on the team that put this participant guide together for personnel of Seminaries and Institutes of Religion, 2008.
9. "History, 1838–1856, volume A-1 [23 December 1805–30 August 1834]," The *Joseph Smith Papers*, 139, accessed December 22, 2020, https://www.josephsmithpapers.org/paper-summary/history-1838-1856-volume-a-1-23-december-1805-30-august-1834/145.

the house of God to help people refine themselves personally and collectively. While in Nauvoo, he and others would hold lengthy meetings and think of big ideas to bring industry, education, and science to their swelling community. So, he understood that Saints had to do their part. He understood that "Jacob," or the body of the Church, covenant Israel, would have to come of age.[10] And that just wasn't the case in his day.

This brings us to today. Nearly 200 years have passed. What is the cultural/social environment today? What is the standing and state of covenant Israel?[11] Are western Missourians still chasing members of The Church of Jesus Christ of Latter-day Saints out of town and out of the state? Of course not. In fact, the state capitol

---

10. "Historian's Office, Martyrdom Account," *The Joseph Smith Papers*, 53, accessed December 22, 2020, https://www.josephsmithpapers.org/paper-summary/historians-office-martyrdom-account/55.
11. Ibid. Joseph declared at Carthage Jail a few hours before his martyrdom: "Our lives have already become jeopardized by revealing the wicked and blood thirsty purposes of our enemies; and for the future we must cease to do so; all we have said about them is truth, but it is not always wise to relate such <all the> truth. Even Jesus the Son of God had to refrain from doing so, and to restrain his feelings many times for the safety of his own person <himself> and those of his followers, and had to conceal the righteous purposes of his heart in relation to many things pertaining to his father's Kingdom. When quite a boy he had all the intelligence necessary to <enable him to> rule and govern the Kingdom of the Jews, and could reason with the wisest and most profound doctors of law and divinity, and make their theories and practice to appear like folly compared with the wisdom he possessed, but he was a boy only, and lacked physical strength even to defend his own person, and was subject to cold, to hunger, and to death. So it is with the Church of Jesus Christ of Latter Day Saints; we have the principles of revelations <of Jesus,> and the knowledge within us is sufficient to organize a righteous government upon the earth, and to give universal peace to all mankind if they will <would> receive it; but we lack the physical strength as did our Savior when a child, to defend our principles, and we shall have of necessity to be afflicted, persecuted, and smitten, and to bear it patiently until Jacob is of age; then he will take care of himself."

has a beautiful room with a mural by Thomas Hart Benton that depicts Missouri's history. A portion of the mural depicts the expulsion of the Latter-day Saints. When on a tour of the capitol, our guide pointed to this part of the mural and said Missourians are not proud of that time in their history.[12] Those who are familiar with Missouri history say the same thing.

What are the lessons we should take from the past 200 years? What about those who still fight, persecute, and destroy no matter what we virtuously become or what we righteously seek out to do? The Lord wanted Zion's Camp (those who went to Jackson County in 1834 with force to reinstate the Saints' upon their rightful lands), to understand one important truth: "I do not require at their hands to fight the battles of Zion; I will fight [their] battles. Behold, the destroyer I have sent forth to destroy and lay waste mine enemies; and not many years hence they shall not be left to pollute mine heritage, and to blaspheme my name upon the lands which I have consecrated for the gathering of my Saints."[13]

I submit that one possible fulfillment of the destroyer being sent is to consider what transpired in the Civil War. Within thirty years ("not many years hence") western Missouri was left in ruins due to multiple factors. Jackson County had become a brutal war zone between the Jayhawkers (abolitionists) and the Bushwhackers (proslavery). The Bushwhackers had been punishing "Union Sympathizers in Jackson County with violent raids on their property, burning their homes and sometimes killing the people." Constant bloodshed was occurring between them and the "unrestrained" Jayhawkers from Kansas. The Union general of the region, Thomas Ewing, "issued Order No. 11" to stop the madness.

This order, itself very extreme, "authorized the military to destroy much of western Jackson, Bates, and Cass Counties (all of

12. Worthy of note is that Governor Christopher S. "Kit" Bond (Missouri) in 1976 rescinded the extermination order issued by Govern Lilburn W. Boogs in 1838.

13. D&C 105:14–15.

which made up the original Jackson County) and there by create a wasteland buffer between Kansas and the rest of Missouri." This left Jackson County in ruin. "A visitor to Jackson County in 1862 described the destruction: 'I went down the Blue River [where I] found houses, barns, outbuildings, nearly all burned down, and nothing left standing but the chimneys.' A history of Missouri adds, 'For a hundred miles, the smoke-stained chimneys, scorched grass, and blackened stumps were all that remained of hard-won homesteads.'"[14]

This isn't just fulfillment of the Lord's words. Joseph Smith told Alexander Doniphan, one of his attorneys during the Liberty Jail saga (1838–1839), that "one day much of Jackson County would be left in ruin. You will live to see the day when [Jackson County] will be visited by fire and sword. . . . The fields and farms and houses will be destroyed, and only the chimneys will be left to mark the desolation."[15] The Lord indicated in June of 1834 (D&C 105) that His enemies would be laid to waste. It was confirmed by His seer five years later. Either by His voice or the voice of His servants it is the same.[16] Alexander would live long enough to witness and read reports of what occurred in Jackson County. He recalled and referred to the whole matter as the "remarkable prediction of the 'Mormon prophet.'"[17]

The Lord will fight battles for Zion.

I suggest that this destruction, this clearing of the inhabitants during the Civil War, began a new era in western Missouri. The large population of the profane were no longer going to "pollute" the region. The Lord saw what was going to unfold. He knew those occupying the land who were contrary to His teachings and Spirit. He knew who would not hear and would not repent. The cultural

14. Lamar C. Berrett and Max H. Parkin, *Sacred Places: Missouri. A Comprehensive Guide to Early LDS Historical Sites*, vol. 4, 67–68.
15. Ibid.
16. D&C 1:38.
17. Berrett, ibid., 68.

and social environment had to be changed. He saw that the land was going to be laid to waste even saying that He "sent forth the destroyer."[18] In fact, a few authors draw attention to the anguish. Seven years before the Civil War began (1855) troubles and bloody conflict exploded in Missouri. Why?

> All the American slave territories that dug in the hardest and whose inhabitants brought upon themselves the most hurt and damage over their efforts to preserve this evil practice (slavery), Missouri ranks number one. Historian David McCullough explained how the Civil War in Missouri began some seven years before it began in the rest of the country: 'it was a war a of plunder, ambush, and unceasing revenge. Nobody was safe. Defenseless towns were burned. . . . Neither then nor later did the rest of the country realize the extent of the horrors.' There is no doubt Satan had set up camp in Missouri years earlier to stomp out any LDS efforts to build Zion—certainly the devil knew it was a promised land designated for Zion. Just because LDS people left years before the Civil War doesn't mean the adversary did. As one eyewitness said: 'the Devil came to the border [state], liked it, and decided to stay awhile.'[19]

After the Civil War, things began to improve—slowly. Not all cultural, racial, and religious prejudices, biases, and jealousies ended immediately. But a spirit of brotherhood and sisterhood began to improve.

From nearly seven years of personal experience (at this writing) I can attest that the state of Missouri is a great place to live.[20] I suppose pockets of prejudice and jealousy exist from those who profane and those pretending to proclaim the gospel. The world has its false priests

---

18. D&C 105:15.
19. This quotation is pulled from Timothy Ballard's book *The Pilgrim Hypothesis*, 183. See also David McCullough's work: *Truman*, 28.
20. My family lives in Columbia, Missouri, about 100 miles east of modern-day Jackson County.

and ministers who oppress and manipulate for gain. There is always a group of people who feel strongly that Latter-day Saints are going to hell. Some religious division obviously prevails. There at still churches contending for converts.[21] One of my former neighbors who was a minister summed up why much of the division and jealousies still occur in some situations and among some churches. "They're constantly counting sheep. It is about money, Ryan." These are his words, not mine.

Nonetheless, could this positive change in the cultural environment reflect more and more people inside and outside Church membership better living the counsel that Joseph Smith gave in 1839? He exhorted all the Saints to "a reformation with one and all, both old and young, teachers and taught, both high and low, rich and poor, bond and free, male and female; let honesty, and sobriety, and candor, and solemnity, and virtue, and pureness, and meekness, and simplicity crown our heads in every place; and in fine, become as little children, without malice, guile or hypocrisy."[22]

When this reformation happens individually, in families, and as a body of covenant people, this is perfection and beauty. Others outside the covenant desire this as well. They seek high standards of activity, morals, honesty, and integrity. There is still a long way to go for all of us. There is plenty of corruption to be found in the center of the land as anywhere in the United States. But the cultural and social climate is better today than it was in the 1830s. Individuals and institutions of all types can buy property, establish businesses and schools, build temples and churches, and peacefully gather and transact business. There are wonderful people in the Midwest who with great sacrifice brought the Sabbath over the Mississippi River. There are many people who are sincerely devoted to serving and worshipping Jesus Christ.

---

21. See Joseph Smith History 1:5–9.
22. "Letter to the Church and Edward Partridge, 20 March 1839," *The Joseph Smith Papers*, 13, accessed March 24, 2021, https://www.josephsmithpapers.org/paper-summary/letter-to-the-church-and-edward-partridge-20-march-1839/13.

The Church has established a respectable foundation among today's social and civil environment. There are approximately 40,000 Latter-day Saints in the greater Kansas City region (the Kansas City Temple district). Around 90,000 people toured the temple during its open house in 2012. Elder Jeremiah Morgan, who at the time of the temple open house was a stake president in Liberty, Missouri, told a newspaper, "The building of any new temple is significant. But certainly, it is close to where Joseph Smith was incarcerated and where many of our 19th century ancestors lived and walked. At minimum, the new temple is an acknowledgement that the community is much different now than it was at that time, and we are grateful to be welcome."[23]

What will be the conditions, culture, and social climate when a more prominent gathering for the New Jerusalem occurs? What possible issues may cause friction (recall the ones of the 1830s)? If the Lord needs to one day do another clearing, it will come by His righteous judgment and His divine timing.

But more important, what will the issues be that unify people? We should acknowledge that the attack on religious freedom in the twenty-first century isn't targeting Catholics and Latter-day Saints as they were in the nineteenth century. The issue of religious freedom may be a powerful unifying issue for different faiths to sustain together. Safety and access to resources may be other reasons for people to be united in large numbers. I also think that people will take notice that the building up of Zion won't be an exclusive thing only for and by Latter-day Saints.

The cultural and social environment is different today then the friction of the 1830s. There surely will be some problems here and there in the future, but the Lord will help fight those battles. Orson Pratt, one of the foundational Saints of Zion, the New Jerusalem, gave practical advice of what he foresaw would happen in coming years:

---

23. Brian Burnes, "New Mormon temple in Kansas City, North, to open in April," *The Kansas City Star*, January 19, 2012.

> Says one, "perhaps they will not allow [us] to purchase the land." The Lord will take care of that; that is in the hands of the Lord. That same being who will assist in the building of a great city on the western boundaries of the state of Missouri, has all power; and when we purchase the land, and go and take possession of it, I do not think we will be driven from our own lands, if we mind our own business and do not meddle with our neighbors' business, and do not undertake to injure them in their rights and privileges, guaranteed to them by the Constitution of our country. If we conduct ourselves in a peaceable manner, I do not see why we may not dwell there as well as other citizens. . . . We will purchase the land, build up cities, towns and villages, build a great capital city, at headquarters, in Jackson County, Missouri. Will we have a temple there? Yes; will we have a beautiful city? Yes, one of the most beautiful cities that will ever be erected on the continent of America will be built up.[24]

As we avoid meddling in our neighbors' business and help one another protect each other's rights and privileges, we will dwell in peace and friendship. We will legally progress. We will build and beautify. We will share and give. We will support and sacrifice. Given the dilapidation in so many areas of our nation this will be welcomed. Our efforts will be a powerful contrast to what has happened over the last several decades. I am not saying it will be easy or without some difficulties here and there, but I do believe our efforts will gladden the hearts and minds of many people. It may seem strange to say, but the conditions of this disintegrating world, caused by a fallen people, will accentuate our efforts in striving for beauty and holiness. Little do we acknowledge that unfolding world events and the fulfillment of prophecies will play to our favor. We will have much to offer. There will be plenty of work to do.

Now, let me conclude this chapter by providing a microscopic illustration of what my family is and has experienced living in Missouri. Living flesh, if you will. It may seem inconsequential to you

---

24. Orson Pratt, *Journal of Discourses* 21:136.

but close to the hearts in our family. When we were living in Utah and preparing to move to Missouri, the neighborhood held a going away party for our family. One neighbor told me before the party that we were going to have a going away party "Missouri style." With "tar and feathers," he said as he laughed. Naturally, we wondered how we would be received into our neighborhood and community. This account about six years later will provide you an answer to how we have been received.

When restrictions due to the coronavirus were placed upon religious gatherings, our neighborhood adjusted a bit. Our different religious meetings we attended regularly had been interrupted. At the time, our family was the only Latter-day Saint family on our side of the neighborhood. Our neighbors are Catholic, Baptist, Lutheran, non-denominational, and I suppose agnostic or indifferent.

Randy, a member of the Baptist faith, decided to hold short Sunday morning devotionals on his front lawn. He invited all from the neighborhood (about thirty came). We sang a few songs, and there was a short message. We attended these Sunday gatherings and really enjoyed visiting and worshipping with our neighbors. After the second week, Randy approached me and said, something like: "Ryan, I am familiar with the Tabernacle Choir and some of their hymns. What hymns can we incorporate next Sunday that would be part of the Mormon way of worshipping?" We discussed a few hymns and what he could play on his piano. Though not an LDS hymn specifically, the following week he played, and we sang, "A Mighty Fortress Is Our God," which is in our hymnbook.[25]

These Sunday gatherings happened for about six weeks.

I have yet to see warm buckets of tar and feathers. We haven't been asked to not come or to leave when we have had neighborhood gatherings or attended events. Several times we have been personally invited to attend their family and church events, and they to ours. To date, neighbors don't want us driven from the street or the city. We are welcome in

25. Martin Luther, "A Mighty Fortress Is Our God," *Hymns,* no. 68.

many of their social settings (even for basketball in their churches). In our neighborhood we help each other with yard projects or bigger chores that need more hands. There seems to be an opposite feeling than in the 1830s. They want us around. They want us involved. We ought to enjoy and become the best neighbors we can possibly be. (In the next chapter I will come back to neighborhoods and neighborliness.) Elder Neil L. Andersen remarked: "In the days ahead, those who believe in Jesus Christ will need the friendship and support of one another."[26]

So, what will the cultural and social environment be like in the future as the New Jerusalem preparation continues to hasten? It's beyond my knowledge. There are a variety of circumstances, people, organizations, and government entities that are out of our control. Nevertheless, the Lord can subdue all things. He will accomplish His work. We can help. Elder Christofferson offered: "There is much we can do as neighbors and fellow citizens to contribute to the sustainability and success of the societies we live in, and surely our most fundamental and enduring service will be to teach and live by the truths inherent in God's great plan of redemption. . . . If enough of us and enough of our neighbors strive to make our decisions and guide our lives by the truth of God, the moral virtues needed in every society will abound."[27]

I choose to push forward with these words from Wilford Woodruff: "We are called upon to work with the Lord just as fast as we are prepared to receive the things of his kingdom. But I am satisfied there has got to be a great change with us in many respects before we are prepared for the redemption of Zion and the building up of the New Jerusalem. I believe the only way for us is to get enough of the Spirit of God that we may see and understand our duties and comprehend the will of the Lord."[28]

The Spirit of the Lord will help us develop greater vision and clearer understanding of our duties. We can begin to comprehend

26. "We Talk of Christ." *Ensign*, Nov. 2020.
27. "Sustainable Societies." *Ensign*, Nov. 2020.
28. Wilford Woodruff, *Journal of Discourses* 16:36.

the will of the Lord as the magnificence of His work moves forward. We can positively affect the cultural and social environment in which we live. This is our preparation. The glory, beauty, and perfection of the New Jerusalem are on the horizon.

> Joseph Smith's description of the region: "The season is mild and delightful nearly three quarters of the year, and as the land of Zion, situated at about equal distances from the Atlantic and Pacific oceans, as well as from the Alleghany and Rocky mountains, in the thirty-ninth degree of north latitude, and between the sixteenth and seventeenth degrees of west longitude, it bids fair—*when the curse is taken from the land—to become one of the most blessed places on the globe.* The winters are milder than the Atlantic states of the same parallel of latitude, and the weather is more agreeable; so that were the virtues of the inhabitants only equal to the blessings of the Lord which He permits to crown the industry of those inhabitants, there would be a measure of the good things of life for the benefit of the Saints, full, pressed down, and running over, even an hundred-fold. . .. When the splendor of the Lord is brought to our consideration for the good of His people, the calculations of men and the vain glory of the world vanish, and we exclaim, 'Out of Zion the perfection of beauty, God hath shined.'"
>
> (*History of the Church*, 1:198. See also www.josephsmithpapers.org; italics for emphasis.)

16

Everyone Knowing Their Neighbor

Zion must increase in beauty and holiness. . . . Every man seeking the interest of his neighbor and doing all things with an eye single to the glory of God.[1]

Everyone has a name, and everyone has a neighbor. We should remember this if we are going to become a holy people and have an inheritance in Zion. The Savior said that in the last days the "love of many [would] wax cold."[2] Thankfully He didn't say the "love of all" would wax cold. There is a door open for each of us to not have our hearts, minds, and actions wax cold. It should be remembered, "every man that will not take his sword against his neighbor must needs flee unto Zion for safety."[3] What might cause this coldness and breakdown in neighborhoods? "To take up the sword against your neighbor doesn't sound like a vast battle

1. D&C 82:14, 19.
2. See Joseph Smith—Matthew 1:8, 30. He emphasizes the idea twice.
3. D&C 45:68.

between hostile nations. . . . This could be conflicts such as civil unrest, neighborhood gang wars, or widespread rioting."[4]

How do we counteract these problems until we are gathered into Zion? Is the answer a little more simple and more genuine than we suppose? I suggest it is.

I want to tell a few stories.

We really can't seek the interests and well-being of one another until we know each other and develop a nature of friendliness. The concepts these stories emphasize are simple, but the terrible reality is they are hard to live for many in our day. We must overcome this before difficult situations are thrust upon us. President Eyring quietly brought attention to the coming days: "We as a people will become more united amid increasing conflict. We will be gathered in the spiritual strength of groups and families filled with gospel light."[5] I firmly believe this isn't just exclusive to members of the Church. Neighbors will join us. We will join them as we seek to obtain and sustain gospel light. Increased conflicts will hasten the gathering.

When our family moved to Missouri in the early summer of 2014, three of our boys were in high school. The youngest boy was in junior high. Imagine the pressure on my wife trying to keep them from boredom, curiosity, and laziness during the day. After a few weeks something needed to be done. We had lawn mowers, and a new Missouri friend graciously allowed us to use his trailer. When we put the two resources together, we had some leverage as parents. Like all *good, mean* parents, we kicked them out the door to distribute flyers for a lawn cutting venture.

They designed the flyers and called themselves "Four Brothers Lawn Care." I knew that for every one hundred homes they passed flyers to they would get about five phone calls. When they were hesitant, we showed them neighborhoods that might yield the most

4. Gerald N. Lund, *The Second Coming of the Lord*, 218.
5. "Prayers of Faith," *Ensign*, May 2020, 28.

calls. Within days they had about ten accounts, with additional customers calling for random cuts here and there. They kept a log of their customers, noting the day they cut and if payment had been received. Most people would call and leave money under their doormats. My sons didn't always see the homeowners.

When I was available, I would help them. When we would pull up to a home, I would say, "What is this customer's name?"

They would say, "Oh, this is the front yard lady."

"Huh?" I said.

"She only wants us to cut her front yard, Dad."

We cut, loaded the machines, and went on to the next house.

"What are these people's names?" I asked.

"This is Spiderman's house." They conveyed he was a young guy just out of college. They couldn't remember his name, but he was always good at paying them immediately and was a cool guy. He paid in cash, so they could never get his name from a check. He had several large spiders on his property, hence, "Spiderman house."

The next house was "Asian Lady." This wasn't in any way derogatory. When they arrived, she would come out and acknowledge them with a wave and put the money under the mat and go back inside. When I showed up with them, I saw her long enough to say, "She's an Asian lady."

Rolling up to the next home, my boys said, "This is Spiderwoman." No relation to Spiderman.

And the next: "This is the mother-in-law house."

"Mother-in-law to whom?" I inquired.

"Some young couple," they said. They had cut a young couple's home a few times, which yielded the mother-in-law referral.

At the next house, one of the boys was sure the customer's name was Frank. Another one of my boys was sure his name was John. The third boy was confident his name was Nick. I knew they couldn't be teasing me, because they got into an argument over who was right. Well, it wasn't settled that day.

At the next house, my oldest son said, "Dad, this guy's name is Gerrick."

I said, "Gerrick. With a 'G'?"

"Yes, with a 'G'."

Another son said, "I think his name is Garrett."

I went with my oldest son.

I began trimming along the front porch. Out came his wife. I introduced myself, and after some small talk, I said, "Where's Gerrick today?"

"Who?" she said.

"Gerrick," I responded.

"You mean Derrick with a 'D'?"

At this point I looked over at one of my boys who had stopped mowing. He just smiled, laughed, and turned away. "Yes, where is Derrick today?"

This could go on and on. PhD Girl. Newell's mother-in-law . . .

By the time we had cut Derrick's lawn, I said, "Boys, let's talk about customer relations." I proceeded to give them some advice and counsel. First on the list was knowing their customers by their proper names. Second, engaging them when they are home and showing kindness and helping with other small tasks they saw that needed to be done. Their customers would appreciate this and probably even give a little extra money here and there.

Within a few weeks, "front yard lady" was Donna. "Spiderman" was Don. "Spiderwoman" was Sharise. Asian Lady was, well, Asian Lady (we only cut her home one or two more times because she moved). The "mother-in-law" was Barbara. And "Gerrick" was Derrick. "Frank" (aka John and Nick) was Tony. Not surprisingly, over the weeks more miscellaneous jobs surfaced around these customers, and more customers came calling.

(Tangentially, I add another principle of a Zion people before I leave lawns. Because I threw a few extra lawns in here and there on my boys, especially for one lady we cut every week, I had to remind them occasionally: "Sometimes you cut lawns for money, and sometimes, you cut lawns." I hope they never forget that.)

For emphasis on my point about knowing names, I share the following.

Writing a piece for the *Boston Globe*, Meaghan McDonough shared her personal account of moving into a three-story apartment building in Dorchester, Massachusetts. Her apartment was on the first floor. She went through the summer, the fall, and winter acknowledging her neighbor, an older lady, with a "smile and a wave." As winter gave way, her neighbor reappeared. She said they continued their smiling and waving to each other. On the other side of the older lady lived a man. Meaghan described him as a man with a mustache who sold flowers at the intersection. ("Mustache man who sells flowers" and "older lady"—sounds like my boys' customers when they first started cutting lawns). Meaghan's own account best tells the ending:

> When spring rolled around, the woman next door returned to her floral throne, I too, became a stoop-sitter. We continued our smiling and waving. But I also started greeting her neighbor with the mustache and the man who sells flowers at the intersection.

I must stop here in her account. "I also started greeting her neighbor." Now we are starting to get somewhere.

> I chatted about the weather with the twins whose apartment shared a porch with mine, and are close to my age. I saw the college boys who lived upstairs enough that when they asked if they could borrow my laundry basket, I said yes. Sometimes, the twins complimented my shoes. The boys upstairs helped me carry in my groceries. . . . Still, I didn't know any of their names, nor they mine. Then, as I sat on the stoop on a sweltering June day, one of the boys asked if he could sit with me while he waited for his girlfriend. "I'm Pablo," he said, smiling as he took a seat. "You're our downstairs neighbor, right?"[6]

Pablo added something to the neighborliness. After nearly a year people started knowing each other's names. It started with a simple young man saying, "I'm Pablo."

---

6. Meaghan McDonough, "We Don't Know Our Neighbors Anymore. Here's What That Costs Us," *Boston Globe*, October 10, 2017.

I don't know Meaghan, but something tells me Pablo does.

I learned the importance of a name from my parents. As noted in the introduction, I was born and reared in Last Vegas, Nevada. When I was four years old, my parents moved into a new home in a new neighborhood. The street was Segovia Terrace, an L-shaped cul-de-sac with twelve homes. As I reflect upon my upbringing, I can honestly say my parents knew everyone on the street by name, including the children. It was a very diverse group of people. Black, white, Asian, a widow, a lesbian couple, varied religious persuasions, single parent homes, along with aging parents living with their married children and grandchildren. Yet my parents knew them all. They also knew several other families who lived on the surrounding streets that led to our cul-de-sac.

Why? How did they do this? What motivated them to do this?

I was excited one day when I found out that one of Evel Knievel's sons had moved into our cul-de-sac. I had seen footage of several of Knievel's daredevil jumps. When I was a boy his action figure was all over the stores. My mother must have given into me one day, because I had one of those figures. Sure enough, I started seeing Evel Knievel visit the home. I always knew when he was there because he had a unique sports car. One day I was riding my bike out of the cul-de-sac and saw him in his son's garage. He was older at the time and long past his dare-devil days. Even in my childhood I could tell he walked with an achiness. I stopped my bike and said, "Mr. Knievel, does your whole body hurt?"

He replied, "Son, if you broke every bone in your body, your body would hurt too."

"Oh," I said, and then I rode off. I was just happy he talked to me.

I referred to the home as Evel Knievel's son's home, or Robbie Knievel's brother's house. My father would remind me that the Knievel who owned the home was Kelly. He had a name, and my parents recognized him as someone just as important as a celebrity. I have learned a lot about being a neighbor since the Segovia Terrace days. And I have learned that not everyone and every street reflects how I grew up. I had a blunt experience a few years back that reminded me this was so.

In Missouri, one of our ecclesiastical leaders asked me to check on the Prince family. Driving into a rural part of Missouri, at night, to find a home in the woods is a bit different than driving in Las Vegas at night. It was dark, and only with the help of modern technology was I able to find the proximity of the home. I found myself on a gravel road in what I call the "jitters." I could see three different trailer homes that lined the same side of this unkept gravel road. Trusting technology, I went to the last of the three, thinking it was the right home. I knocked. A man in his fifties answered. "Is this the Prince home?" I inquired.

"No," he said. "I don't know them, and never heard of them." I thanked him and went back to my car.

Google maps was telling me I was in the right place. But this man knew nothing of the Prince family. Before assuming they had moved and the address was incorrect, I thought I would knock on the home next door. It wasn't far. I could have thrown a baseball from the porch I had just left and easily hit the home. I could see it through the brush and trees. Maybe the occupants of this home knew of the Prince family and their whereabouts. I pulled into their driveway and approached the front door. I knocked and inquired. A woman in her sixties said, "Yes, this is the Prince home. Come in."

I told them I had accidently first approached their neighbors. She conveyed that they didn't know their neighbors. "Well," I said, "I discovered that your neighbors don't know you either."

I marveled at this. So close, yet so distant. They just readily let me in without hesitation (I suppose because I told them I was from the Church) but had no idea who their neighbors were. Honestly, this experience saddened me. I know it is more common than we would think. But this cannot be. This personal indifference or isolation will not be, cannot be, the situation in Zion. There will be respect of time and property, of space and personality, but Zion's inhabitants will be friendly and anxiously engaged with one another. The sociality will be a stark contrast to what we witness in today's neighborhoods and dwellings.

Over the years I have tried to instill into our children and my students this simple rule: Know your neighbors two doors down—

each way—both sides of the street. For you, it might be two apartment doors down—each way—both sides of the hall. For others it could be two farms down—each way—both sides of the county road. I think you get my point.

We must know our neighbors. They must know us. If we lived this simple approach of two doors down, each way, both sides of the street, we could be a remarkably connected world. A much friendlier world. Compassion may surface more than contention. Knowing our neighbors will be so natural and genuine for a Zion people.

But what gets in the way today?

Because of broad circumstances that each of us are born into or have thrust upon us in this life, many of us choose to live under a variety of labels, titles, and platforms. Yet, neighbor, one of the important ones, is being ignored. In a day of caricature and insult, sincere neighbor-to-neighbor interactions and awareness can become a welcome respite. Virtues like sociality and kindness, along with consideration and helpfulness, will flourish. Genuine people with moral guidance can contribute to neighborliness. It ought to start in the home and very close to home. Regarding COVID-19, President Nelson asked: "Has this shared trial drawn you closer to your neighbors—to your brothers and sisters across the street and around the world?"[7]

It seems like the labels people want to live under are the least significant and most problematic. Professional, social, political, and even religious labels, roles, and titles rule the day. In many instances, labels ruin the day. We clamor for special interest attention but shun sincere neighbor interest. We are vocal in our image-driven and attention-grabbing society which seeks the approval of someone not only on the other side of a screen but in another part of the world. Tragically, we are indifferent with those who live next door.

When we look past roles and labels emphasized in scripture—child, son or daughter, parent, husband and wife, father and

7. "What We Are Learning and Will Never Forget," April 2021 general conference.

> Joseph Smith: "The advancement of the cause of God and the building up of Zion is as much one man's business as another's. The only difference is, that one is called to fulfill one duty, and another duty; 'but if one member suffers, all the members suffer with it, and if one member is honored all the rest rejoice with it, and the eye cannot say to the ear, I have no need of thee, nor the head to the foot, I have no need of thee;' party feelings, separate interests, exclusive designs should be lost sight of in the one common cause, in the interest of the whole." ("History, 1838–1856, volume C-1 [2 November 1838–31 July 1842]," p. 1327, The Joseph Smith Papers, accessed June 28, 2021).

mother, or neighbor and friend—the cold front in human relations bears down upon us. We wax cold as the Savior prophesied. We should reconsider the polarizing labels and identifiers that we choose to live out our lives. If we can choose to live in our role as a neighbor, we can minimize the contention and anger trying to make greater in-roads into our society. This will require that we seek the interest of our neighbors. This will require that we be friendly neighbors ourselves. That we know each other's names.

In our married life, my wife and I have lived in an apartment complex, a basement apartment, rented homes, a townhouse that we owned, and two different residential homes. We have lived in Nevada, Utah, and Missouri. I feel like we have had a rich exposure to people in general and broad experiences with neighbors. We have come and gone, and many neighbors have come and gone. It has hopefully given us opportunities to become more neighborly.

Being neighborly is a practical principle to govern our lives by. It will help gather Israel, spiritually and literally. It will be a distinguishing characteristic of a Zion people.

17

Mary Ann Young—Where to Be and Who to Follow

"We shall see the New Jerusalem coming down from God in heaven to join with the Holy City we have built."[1]

In chapter 1, I asked: In a book about a holy city to be prepared and built up by the Lord and His people in the last days, why would I draw attention to Emma Hale Smith? At the end of this compilation, I ask: In a book about a holy city to be prepared and built up by the Lord and His people in the last days, why would I draw attention to Mary Ann Young?

I will share a crucial point in Mary Ann Young's life and let you draw some conclusions.

Mary Ann Young[2] made two significant choices in 1840. One had to do with where to live. The other, who to follow. She made

1. Bruce R. McConkie. "The Coming Tests and Trials and Glory," *Ensign*, May 1980.
2. Mary was Brigham Young's second wife. He married her in March 1834. His first wife, Miriam, died in 1832.

these choices while her husband, Brigham Young, was absent on his eighth mission (on his way to England). When he left in the fall of 1839, Mary and four small children were living in abandoned military barracks in Montrose, Iowa. These were difficult circumstances, even by early American frontier standards. The danger, darkness, and want for necessities of life must have challenged her mental capacity. She learned to endure despair and anxiety.

Her fortitude was exhibited in late November 1839. Sick with malaria and with a northwest storm bearing down upon her back, she took a skiff and rowed across the Mississippi River with a two-month-old babe strapped to her by a blanket. The three oldest children—crying for food—were left at the barracks. She returned several hours later with a few potatoes and a little flour. Cold and extremely wet, her tenacity alleviated her children's hunger.[3]

Across the Mississippi River to the east, a larger number of Latter-day Saints were gathering in a place renamed Nauvoo. Particularly notable among them was the Prophet Joseph Smith and his family. But circumstances weren't much better in Nauvoo. The temporal quagmire Mary and others found themselves in mirrored the marshy land they were physically occupying. Where to go, where to live, and what to do must have been pressing her mind (and others' minds) nearly every waking hour.[4]

On his way to England, Brigham Young passed through Kirtland, Ohio. While there, he learned that his wife's father, James

---

3. Emmeline B. Wells, "Biography of Mary Ann Angell Young," *Juvenile Instructor*, Jan. 1, 1891, 57.
4. One author has penned this tender reflection of Mary Ann: "Latter-day Saint pioneer Mary Ann Angell Young was a living testament that faith in God and his gospel is reason enough to endure any number of hardships with dignity, patience, and unwavering hope. So deep and steady was her devotion to the gospel that no extremity of persecution, toil, illness, or separation from loved ones in life or in death disturbed her faith. She endured countless trials and privations not by dint of sheer stoic resignation, but with a tempered and whole-souled trust in the Lord" (Rex G. Jensen, "Indomitable Mary Ann," *Ensign*, July 1993).

William Angell, had requested that his daughter and her mother return to Kirtland. There they could live in better circumstances.[5]

Mary Ann Young had some choices to make. She could stay in the barrack situation in Iowa with very little food, or return to Kirtland, where her father could alleviate her worries about food and shelter. Initially Brigham Young welcomed the thought of her returning to Kirtland. He had hoped to see her and spend time with her before he departed across the waters in the late spring.[6] But he was not entirely informed to her feelings nor the counsel she had received from the Prophet Joseph Smith and other Church leaders.

Sometime in the spring of 1840 Brigham Young learned that his wife had "given up going to Kirtland." He also learned that Joseph Smith was trying to arrange for a home to be built for her near the temple lot up on the bluff. Though comforted that his family had an option out of the barracks, Brigham conveyed to Mary his desire: "I would rather you would have a house on my lot that br joseph [*sic*] set apart for me near his own house."[7] The property he was referring to was down from the bluff on the flats, three blocks north and one block west of Joseph Smith's residence. With the start of a log cabin on this property, and with her husband's input, Mary Ann moved forward in faith. The proximity would yield and refine significant relationships and complement the divinely orchestrated events in Church leadership yet to unfold.

Brigham Young was pleased that his wife had made the decision to stay with the Lord's "counselors."[8] Her decision may have been

---

5. Ronald O. Barney, "Letter of a Missionary Apostle to His Wife: Brigham Young to Mary Ann Angell Young, 1839–1841," 166. *BYU Studies* Volume 38: no. 2 (1999): 156–201.
6. Ibid. Brigham Young even suggested some homes she might be able to occupy with the help of Oliver Granger, a church agent settling affairs for Joseph Smith and others in Kirtland. He was on his way to the British Isles.
7. Ibid., 177.
8. See D&C 112:20. The Lord told the body of the Church in an 1837 revelation that "whoso receiveth me, receiveth those, the First Presidency, whom I have sent, whom I have made *counselors* for my name's sake unto you" (italics for emphasis).

a reminder and a strength to his own resolve to always do likewise. He dropped the idea of her coming back to Ohio and praised her: "[*sic*] I heard you was not going to Kirtland. I am rejoiced to think you are willing to szacrefise everithing for the councel of our brotherin that the lord has given ous for Counceleas [counselors] in these last days it is my feelings to goe right strate ahead if it takes all the hare of my head. I want to live in that way that the lord will say by in by to me when he comes you have well don now you mad [may] enjoi the socity of your family . . . I will mak you a ruler over much."[9]

President Henry B. Eyring: "You sisters, your daughters, your granddaughters, and the women you have nurtured will be at the heart of creating that society of people who will join in glorious association with the Savior. You will be an essential force in the gathering of Israel and in the creation of a Zion people who will dwell in peace in the New Jerusalem" ("Sisters in Zion," Ensign, Nov. 2020).

In Mary Ann, Brigham had a like-minded wife. She wanted to follow the Lord's appointed servants in her day. The Prophet Joseph Smith, the priesthood and priesthood keys, and her faithful friends had moved on from their labors in Kirtland. Mary Ann chose not to go back to Kirtland. Her great sacrifice is an example of following the Savior and claiming His promise. "And every one that hath forsaken houses, or brethren, or sisters, or father, or mother, or wife or children, or lands, for my name's sake, shall receive an hundredfold and shall inherit everlasting life."[10] Mary Ann Young was equal to Emma Smith. She proved to forsake all that the Lord requested.

Because of his wife's remarkable resolve to live by her covenants, Brigham Young was right where he wanted to be when he returned

9. Ronald O. Barney, "Letter of a Missionary Apostle to His Wife: Brigham Young to Mary Ann Angell Young, 1389–1841," 177–178. *BYU Studies* Volume 38: no. 2 (1999): 156–201.

10. Matthew 19:29.

home from the British Isles. He was right where he needed to be. By putting his shoulders behind a wheel barrel and his hands on the trowel, he eventually moved from a log home into a brick home on the property.[11] A home that would become a pivotal gathering place as the transition from Joseph's presiding position as President of the Church fell collectively upon the Quorum of the Twelve of Apostles. Mary Ann's resolve to stay where the keys of the priesthood resided was crucial to what was coming.

Six weeks after the death of Joseph and Hyrum Smith, Brigham returned to Nauvoo from a mission in the eastern United States. Three days later, a majority of the Quorum of the Twelve Apostles and other Church leaders began meeting in the east room of the brick home. They immediately addressed the temporal affairs of the Church. They gathered to hold prayer meetings, asking the Lord to deliver them "from the mob" and to restore the health of the sick. On Thursday, August 15, a meeting was held and "many matters were talked over." But of great importance this day was the determination of the Apostles. At this time, they had "resolved to bear off the kingdom of God in all the world, in truth, honesty, virtue and holiness."[12]

Important decisions at this time had to be made concerning those Church officials who did not entirely understand that charge or who did not want to do it under the keys of the Twelve Apostles. For example, John E. Page and Lyman Wight (members of the Twelve), George Miller, and of course Sydney Rigdon, who told Brigham Young that he had "power and authority above the Twelve Apostles and did not consider himself amenable to their counsel."[13] This may have been in protest of what Brigham had told the Saints

11. Brigham Young noted at the end of May 1843 that he moved his family into the brick home.
12. *History of the Church* 7:249 (see pages 247–250 for the initial meetings at Brigham Young's home).
13. Ibid. 7:267. John F. Boynton and William Smith would also have to be considered as indifferent and/or rejecting the Twelve.

about three weeks earlier in Sidney's hearing. "You cannot take Elder Rigdon and place him above the Twelve; if so, he must be ordained by them."[14]

Notwithstanding Elder Rigdon's claims, the following two brief entries from Brigham Young convey how most of the Saints felt at this time. On September 19, 1844 he states: "At home waiting upon my wife who was very sick. The *Saints called upon me for counsel and direction.*" The next day he added: *"Attending to ordinances in behalf of the Saints, and laying hands on the sick.* The Lord is with me continually."[15]

Most of the Saints understood and relied on the restored truth that "God [gave] priesthood authority and priesthood keys to servants who could act in His name for the salvation and edification of all of His children."[16] Though Mary, Brigham, and other early Latter-day Saints may have expressed different language, they understood and governed their lives by the following doctrine: "Jesus Christ holds all the keys of the priesthood pertaining to His Church. He has conferred upon each of His Apostles all the keys that pertain to the kingdom of God on earth. The President of the Church is the only person authorized to exercise all of those priesthood keys."[17] The First Presidency are "counselors" for Jesus Christ.[18]

Mary understood this. She, Brigham, and their dear friends in the covenant didn't want to sever themselves from Jesus Christ,

---

14. Ibid., 7:233. Brigham was a little forward in his August 8, 1844, discourse. He asked matter-of-factly, "Do you want the church properly organized, or do you want a spokesman to be chief cook and a bottle-washer. . . . Does this Church want it as God organized it? Or do you want to clip the power of the priesthood, and let those who have the keys of the priesthood go and build up the kingdom in all the world, where the people will hear them?" (234–235).
15. Ibid., 7:273–274; emphasis added.
16. Doctrinal Mastery Core Document, *Priesthood and Priesthood Keys.* Seminaries and Institutes of Religion, 2017.
17. Ibid.
18. D&C 112:20.

Joseph Smith His servant, or His ordained Apostles. Being faithful and loyal to those leaders given priesthood keys was akin to staying close to Jesus Christ. It is He that gives His appointed servants the right to govern and direct the affairs of His Church. "Priesthood keys are necessary to direct the preaching of the gospel and the administration of the ordinances of salvation."[19] Mary saw this firsthand in her brick home in Nauvoo.

The work that unfolded in the east room of this home had three major objectives. Each objective aligned with the Lord's purposes and promises in the Last Days. First, to finish the temple so the ordinances of salvation could be extended. Second, continue to send servants to the four corners of the world to preach the gospel and invite Israel to be gathered. Third, prepare to take the Lord's covenant people into the wilderness, to a place prepared and designated by God (and build up a conglomerate of stakes of Zion).[20] Whenever the Apostles gathered in the east room, their purposes were to see those three objectives through. They did so by exercising priesthood keys.

Mary and Brigham Young's home in Nauvoo is a modest historical landmark to the Latter-day Saints. What happened in their home (east wing) is a significant eternal landmark to The Church of Jesus Christ of Latter-day Saints. What happened in their home in August and September 1844 was a time that solidified the doctrine of priesthood and priesthood keys into the hearts of most of the first generation of Latter-day Saints.[21]

This trusting in priesthood keys is what led Mary Ann Young to sacrifice all things and follow the Lord's "counselors" in the Last

---

19. Ibid.
20. See Revelation 12:6. Read Revelation 12:1–6. Wandle Mace believed the building of the Nauvoo Temple was preparing the Saints for a fulfillment of these verses. The exterior of the temple even reflected Revelation 12:1. See his reminisces. In BYU Collections.
21. The author acknowledges the Seventies Hall and the Temple were also important places where these doctrines of priesthood and priesthood keys were taught and emphasized.

Days. She won her contest of faith. She was a woman of great spiritual stamina who exercised great faith at a crucial time in the Restoration. In 1840 she knew where to be and who to follow. For these two reasons she will be called "the Friend of God."[22] For these two reasons her eternal family will have no end.

Like Emma Smith, Mary Ann will have her inheritance in Zion, the New Jerusalem. And so will we if we remember where to be and who to follow.

How does Mary's story relate to our preparation for the coming New Jerusalem? What personal lessons may you take away from this account as you consider the themes and concepts presented in this book?

---

22. James 2:23.

Conclusion

"Zion is a return to a former state of existence . . . . But the world as we know it is the very antithesis of Zion."[1]

Is it all a dream? Gerald N. Lund wrote, "The implications [New Jerusalem] has for members of the Church sometime in the future is so incredible that at times it may seem to be more of a dream than a reality."[2]

It *is* a reality.

There will always be those who mock the idea of a New Jerusalem. Or those who don't believe it will ever happen, or who are entirely indifferent. Even so, the evidence of the New Jerusalem's reality is steadily compounding. We have the revelations in the Doctrine and Covenants to confirm it. We have modern-day revelation that confirms it.[3] We have multiple generations of righteous families who "looked for a city . . . whose builder and maker [was] God." These righteous families believed in the promises even though they

1. Hugh Nibley, *Approaching Zion*, 11, 248.
2. Gerald N. Lund, *The Second Coming of the Lord*, 233–234. This sentence was pulled from his book. In context, Elder Lund was strongly making the case of its reality. In his book *The Second Coming of the Lord*, he gives over fifty pages to the City of Zion, the New Jerusalem.
3. See Russell M. Nelson, "The Future of the Church: Preparing the World for the Savior's Second Coming," *Ensign*, April 2020,13–17.

never received them in mortality.[4] The Lord has promised them full compensation.

After the Flood, many righteous families sought to join the translated city of Enoch. Many longed to follow the path of the city of Salem, who most likely joined the city of Enoch.[5] Many knew by prophecy that in the last days there would be a New Jerusalem. Their hope, their desires, their patience was obtaining a heavenly city. The New Jerusalem will be a monument to their hopes and desires that carried them through their mortal tribulation. Jesus Christ will stand among a people who would have Him to be their God. He has prepared a city for them.[6] He has prepared a city for us.

These two glorious cities will have a divine blending under the guiding hand of the Lord. Enoch's Zion society will descend with great joy. Imagine the stories, the power, the example they will have to present to those who are in the New Jerusalem. They will "receive" those Saints in the New Jerusalem "into [their] bosom." Imagine the unification of such a people. Imagine the genuine and undefiled nature of those eternal relationships. The Son of God will make an "abode" there and "for the space of a thousand years the earth shall rest."[7]

The New Jerusalem will be one of two world capitals. From it, the law shall go forth. In the New Jerusalem, the fundamental unity of society—a Zion society—will be the family. "Righteous men and women shall oversee their own families in all matters, and they shall preside as kings and queens, priests and priestesses. A theocracy will be reinstituted, and Jesus will reign as King of kings and Lord of lords."[8] Fatherhood and motherhood will beautifully demonstrate godhood, the antithesis of current day trends.

---

4. See Hebrews 11:10–15.
5. JST, Genesis 14:32–34.
6. Hebrews 10:16.
7. Moses 7:63–65.
8. Robert L. Millet and Joseph Fielding McConkie, *Joseph Smith: The Choice Seer,* chapter 32.

But what will happen before that day? What will mortal men have to pass through? What will the disciples and true Saints of Jesus Christ pass through? Enoch saw that there would be "great tribulations among the *wicked*."[9] Surely not all man-made disturbances and alarming injustices provoked by the wicked will bypass every righteous person.[10] But the Lord has made it known in word and in power that He will not always allow the wicked to destroy the righteous. He can and will preserve the righteous, "even by fire."[11]

We should anticipate an accelerating of events. Events of the past few years seem to indicate that we are on the front end of an accelerated pace of incidents and prophecy being fulfilled. Elder Neal A. Maxwell saw what was ahead for us: "Mark well what kind of days they will be, days when, *with special visibility*, the Lord will 'make bare his holy arm in the eyes of all the nations'. . . . There will be *a compression of events*. . . . Only those in the process of becoming the men and women of Christ will be able to keep their spiritual balance."[12] Elder Maxwell's words resonate with the words of President Russell M. Nelson in his ministry.

A compression of events? Think on that! Does the idea that there will be a compression of events scare you or excite you? Or both?

The New Jerusalem must be organized, constructed, and sustained by a people who sincerely desire to live by celestial law. Bruce R. McConkie taught, "And after it is built, the fear and dread of the Lord will rest upon the wicked as they see how and in what

---

9. Moses 7:66; emphasis added.
10. Alma 14:10–11 is a very tender and difficult story that reminds us of this fact.
11. 1 Nephi 22:16–17. This could be dual, literally by fire and by the fire of the Holy Ghost. There are examples of both.
12. "My Servant Joseph," *Ensign*, May 1992. President Nelson also said recently: "This is a hinge point in the history of the Church. Things are going to move forward at an accelerated pace. . . . The Church is going to have an unprecedented future. Unparalleled. We're just building up to what's ahead" ("LDS President Russell M. Nelson Gives Special Invitation on Bicentennial of First Vision," *Daily Herald*, January 3, 2020).

manner the Lord preserves its righteous inhabitants."[13] Jesus Christ is an unmatched Deliverer from spiritual and physical death.[14] This will be magnificently clear in the New Jerusalem. In the meantime, He graciously extends fortitude to those who desire it. He helps us keep our spiritual balance on the covenant path.

As scattered Israel are gathered and choose the covenant path, His power will be displayed in a never-before-seen way.[15] The Lord has the New Jerusalem and countless other places, like Jerusalem of old, and stakes of Zion, for those who desire to be taught in His ways and walk in His paths.[16] Unique places of refuge and places of safety will be designated and governed by Him, even while the "devil has power over his own dominion."[17] But his power is coming to an end. The "chastening hand of an Almighty God" has a "consumption decreed." There will be a "full end of all nations."[18]

In the meantime, we must confront that places, things, and people need to be renewed, cleaned up, and changed from head to foot, so to speak. This doesn't sit well with many of us. It means change. The world is fallen and so are we. The evidence isn't in our favor. There needs to be a cleansing, both physically and spiritually. There needs to be an understanding and quest for perfection of beauty.[19]

The perfection of beauty will be exhibited from New Jerusalem. It will be one of the "holy places" where people can "stand" with Jesus Christ and everything He represents.[20] A place where we can prepare for the "hour of judgment."[21]

---

13. Bruce R. McConkie, *Millennial Messiah: The Second Coming of the Son of Man*, 303.
14. D&C 138:23.
15. Jeremiah 16:14–15.
16. See Isaiah 2:3.
17. Consider D&C 1:35–36.
18. D&C 87:6.
19. Psalm 50:2.
20. See D&C 45:32, 87:8.
21. D&C 88:84.

Elder Christofferson has spoken often about the theme of establishing a Zion people capable of building a holy city. He suggests for a Zion people to organize themselves a few things will need to happen. We will need to "become unified in one heart and one mind . . . to become, individually and collectively, a holy people . . . and to care for the poor and needy with such effectiveness that we eliminate poverty among us. We cannot wait until Zion comes for these things to happen—Zion will come only as they happen. . . . To come to Zion, it is not enough for you or me to be somewhat less wicked than others. We are to become not only good but holy men and women."[22]

That holiness comes with great self-restraint. Again, the antithesis of much what we see from inhabitants in the world. As Orson F. Whitney prepared the *The Life of Heber C. Kimball* for publication, he contemplated the ideal of Zion. As he wrote about the city of Zion being delayed for a little season he stated: "The redemption of Zion is more than a purchase or recovery of lands, the building of cities, or even the founding of nations. It is the conquest of the heart, the subjugation of the soul, the sanctifying of the flesh, the purifying and ennobling of the passions."[23]

This is personal. This is real. The Lord cannot bring about a holy city with profane individuals. They must be striving for the refinement of the heart, the spirit, the body, and the mind.

We may never see the city in mortality. It lies at an undesignated future date. But we should see and experience a personal conquest over sin, false philosophies, and wrong traditions. Elder David R. Stone noticed: "We seldom realize the extent to which we are a product of the culture of our place and time. . . . We do not need to become as puppets in the hands of the culture of the place and time."[24]

---

22. D. Todd Christofferson, "Come to Zion," *Ensign*, Nov. 2008.
23. *The Life of Heber C. Kimball*, 65. Suggest contemplating his continued words on page 66 as well.
24. David R. Stone, "Zion In the Midst of Babylon," *Ensign*, May 2006.

Little does the world know who the deceiving puppeteer is who holds the strings. A holy and clean city of both environment and citizens is maddening to him. Whereas the Lord sustains perfection and beauty of person and place, the adversary sustains the mediocrity and repulsiveness of person and place. We are up against some very blatant and threatening obstacles that attempt to ruin us and the Lord's purposes. Babylon doesn't like what is on the horizon for the people of God. We can expect our liberties to be suspended and our welfare to be threatened. The Lord said that we would be in "bondage" and that the redemption of Zion will need to "come by power."[25]

On the bookshelf of lost scripture there is a volume entitled *The Book of the Wars of the Lord*.[26] Something ought to have been compiled on the subject. The Lord gave His promise that He would fight for Zion and His Saints.[27] He promised that no weapon formed against His servants and people would prosper.[28] Biblical accounts assure us that Jehovah protected and gave victory to His people when they were obedient and justified before Him.[29] *The Book of the Wars of the Lord* will accentuate known and unknown accounts of the Lord fighting battles for His covenant people.

It would be nice to have it on our bookshelves. Perhaps a reading of the accounts would restrain men and their appetite for war. Perhaps reading about Jehovah's power to cause the sun and the moon to stand still, or to rain massive hailstones from heaven, would subdue man's penchant to fire up modern day mechanisms of war. President Spencer W. Kimball asked this question and added the following observation:

---

25. D&C 103:15–17.
26. Numbers 21:14. There are more than fifteen books mentioned in the Bible that are not canonized. For references and further understanding of lost scripture, see "Lost Books" LDS Bible Dictionary [2013].
27. Isaiah 31:4; D&C 105:14.
28. See Isaiah 54:17; 3 Nephi 22:17; D&C 71:9; 109:25.
29. "Jehovah is the premortal Jesus Christ and came to earth being born of Mary" (see "Jehovah," LDS Bible Dictionary [2013]).

"I hope we are all familiar with these words of the Lord and with his predictions concerning other coming events, such as the building of the New Jerusalem and the redemption of the old, the return of Enoch's Zion, and Christ's millennial reign.
"Not only do I hope that we are familiar with these coming events, I hope also that we keep the vision of them continually before our minds. This I do because upon a knowledge of them, and an assurance of their reality and a witness that each of us may have part therein, rests the efficacy of Christ's admonition, 'be not trouble.'"

(In Conference Report, Oct. 1966, 51–52).

"Why must men rely on physical fortification and armaments when the God of heaven yearns to bless them? One stroke of his omnipotent hand could make powerless all nations who oppose, and save a world even when in its death throes. Yet men shun God and put their trust in weapons of war, or in the 'arm of flesh.'"[30]

It is the "arm of the flesh" or the Lord's stretched-out arm.[31] It is the hard-hearted camp or the soft-hearted camp. It is carelessness or perfection. It is perverseness or virtue and beauty. It is Babylon or Zion.

Why would we look to a holy city in the future as an ideal and pattern to live out our days in Babylon? "We seek Zion because it is the habitation of our Lord, who is Jesus Christ, our Savior and Redeemer. In Zion and from Zion, His luminous and

30. Spencer W. Kimball, *The Miracle of Forgiveness* (Salt Lake City: Bookcraft, 1969), 318.
31. Alma 62:41. "I think it safe to say that when people turn from a sense of accountability to God and begin to trust instead in the "arm of flesh," disaster lurks. Trusting in the arm of flesh is to ignore the divine Author of human rights and human dignity and to give highest priority to riches, power, and the praise of the world (while often mocking and persecuting those who follow a different standard)" (D. Todd Christofferson, *Ensign*, Nov. 2020).

incandescent light will shine forth, and He will rule forever."[32]

Can you see the luminous and incandescent light on the horizon? It is a city, a holy city—the New Jerusalem. The Lord is in the very details. There is no uncertainty here. It is a reality. Our Savior Jesus Christ has spoken. It will come to pass.

President Marion G. Romney (1897–1988) said: "It was in the light of Christ's foreknowledge . . . that he said to his disciples, 'be not troubled'."

32. David R. Stone, "Zion In the Midst of Babylon," *Ensign*, May 2006. I'll make note here that the Lord said he would favor Zion and call upon the kings, rulers, presidents, governors, and so on in the world "to give heed to the light and glory of Zion." See D&C 124:3–7.

Appendix A

Random Questions and Answers, Possible Answers, and No Answers

What are some of the direct and indirect names of the New Jerusalem we find referenced in ancient and modern scripture?

"The city of the Lord. The Zion of the Holy One of Israel" (Isaiah 60:14). "The city of our God" (D&C 97:19). "Sought out. A City not forsaken" (Isaiah 62:12). Zion or Mount Zion (D&C 84:2). "Holy City" or "His Tabernacle" (Moses 7:62). "The perfection of beauty" (Psalms 50:2). "Joy of the whole earth" (Psalm 48:2). "The city of righteousness, the faithful city" (Isaiah 1:26). "The city of our solemnities" (Isaiah 33:20). "The kingdom of Zion" (D&C 105:32).

Is there any significance or symbolism in the New Jerusalem being designated in the same spot as the Garden of Eden?

As I mentioned in chapter 2, this region in western Missouri has a storied past, a relatively quiet present, and a delightful future. From a holy garden to a holy city, the region has been under the Lord's direct care for thousands of years. There must be some interest and reason the New Jerusalem will occupy the territory where the Garden of Eden was located. The land was then, and the land will be, in the days of the New Jerusalem cultivated and beautified. This isn't an answer to the question (I'll let you come up with your own answer), but President Joseph Fielding Smith simply stated: "We should be grateful to the Prophet Joseph Smith because of the revelation which the Lord gave him pointing out the place of the Garden of Eden, and to give us the information that when the earth is restored, as it surely will be, the great city New Jerusalem will be in the place where Eden was" (see *Answers to Gospel Questions*, 4:24; Isaiah 51:3).

Is the significant and specific return of ten lost tribes from the land of the "north countries" have any connection with the New Jerusalem?

The language of the revelations in D&C 133:26–34 and Jeremiah 31:6–12 strongly indicate there is. Elder Gerald Lund explained that the gathering of Israel is a "general process" and that the gathering of a ten lost tribes is a "specific return" or event (see *The Second Coming of the Lord*, 256–264). They are leaving somewhere and going to gather somewhere else. I believe this is Zion, the New Jerusalem. "There shall be a day, that the watchmen upon the mount Ephraim shall cry, Arise ye, and let us go up to Zion unto the Lord our God," Jeremiah recorded. "They shall come and sing in the height of Zion, and shall flow together to the goodness of the LORD," he continued. Covenant people of all tribes of Israel (especially those considered of the ten lost tribes) will come to Zion. The revelation given to Joseph Smith emphasizes the Lord's direct care in getting His covenant people to Zion. As alluded to in the conclusion, as scattered Israel are gathered and choose the covenant path, His power will be displayed in a never-before-seen way. Jeremiah again has something to say on the subject (see Jeremiah 16:14–15).

What other event (or events) may signify the building up of the city of Zion, the New Jerusalem?

If purchasing land is considered part of the building up of the city, then that began in 1831. Maybe it is helpful to consider some significant events with these questions. Does the buildup of the city and the initial gathering of people come before or after Adam-Ondi-Ahman occurs? Will construction and gathering begin before the Millennium (during the seven thousand years of the earth's temporal existence)? Will it happen before or after *the times of the Gentiles* being fulfilled? (See JST Luke 21: 24–26, 32). Will the city be started before the land masses are brought back into the place they were before the earth was divided? (See D&C 133:22–24). Will it be in a time of peace or great turmoil under which it will be built? One thing to consider is a revelation given in September 1832, which directly stated that the city of New Jerusalem would be "built, beginning at the temple lot." The temple lot that was dedicated by Joseph Smith in the summer of 1831 (see D&C 84:2–4). Could building a temple(s) at this "temple lot" be, symbolically speaking, the cornerstone of the city? (Like cornerstones we place to symbolize the beginning of the construction of a building?) The "when" was addressed in chapter 3.

Is there a simultaneous reclamation and buildup of Jerusalem of Old and the New Jerusalem?

Orson Pratt said there is a time difference of the cities receiving the Lord's light and power: "The light of Zion [New Jerusalem] is to come, and the glory of the Lord is to arise upon her, *before* wickedness is destroyed from among the nations; whereas Jerusalem is not to become holy, and the glory of God is not to arise upon her, *until* the Lord comes and destroys wickedness, and converts the Jews" (*New Jerusalem of the Fulfillment of Modern Prophecy* [pamphlet] [Liverpool, England: October 1, 1849], 42.)

Will the city of Enoch occupy the same land and spot as the New Jerusalem built up by Saints of the Last Days?

Remember that land masses are going to be adjusted—a lot. The city of Enoch *could* itself be placed as a distinct place of land, independent of the city built up by the Saints : (I am aware that there is a unique statement in Wilford Woodruff's journal about the city of Enoch. He recorded that when Enoch's city was translated it left the void on the earth we know as the Gulf of Mexico. His journal indicates Brigham Young said this and that Brigham heard it from Joseph Smith. But remember, this is the only source suggesting Joseph Smith taught that. At least to my knowledge. If true, it does place Enoch's city—in Zion—which Joseph Smith said was all north and south America.) The revelation says, "Enoch . . . and all [his] city" will meet the inhabitants of the New Jerusalem. This could be referencing the people of the city not the city itself. Regardless, the glorious association and interaction is more important than physical location of the cities. The assimilation of the two cities will be marvelous. Another revelation says Enoch and "his brethren, Who were separated from the earth, and were received unto myself—a city reserved until a day of righteousness shall come" (D&C 45:11–12).

Who will be among the inhabitants of the city of New Jerusalem descending from heaven?

The City of Enoch, and perhaps a host of others who were translated prior to and after the flood. This could include those of Melchizedek's city, Salem. The Joseph Smith Translation of Genesis 14:25–40 seems to indicate they were translated. (But perhaps they will occupy another land and dwell near Old Jerusalem. I don't know.) It seems more reasonable to say that any celestial being will be or can be welcome in the city of New Jerusalem. A sub question here is, will the status of translated beings come to an end at this point? I don't know. But Joseph Smith did teach that "translated bodies cannot enter into their rest until they have undergone a change equivalent to death" (*History of the Church* 4:425).

Do portions of New Jerusalem have entrance qualifications distinct from entrance qualifications to the borders of the sovereignty of Zion?

In my mind there seems to be a distinction between the Land of Zion and the New Jerusalem within the Land of Zion. Jesus Christ will not make His abode there until He comes with Enoch and his people. Will this city of God be an exalted abode within a terrestrial abode of the earth? The earth sometime in the Millennium will be "renewed and receive its paradisiacal glory." Its condition will be like unto the Garden of Eden (see Articles of Faith 1:10 and footnote). There will be communion with mortal and immortal beings. "Because of the destruction of the wicked at the Savior's Second Coming, only righteous people will live on the earth at the beginning of the Millennium. They will be those who have lived virtuous and honest lives. These people will eventually inherit either the terrestrial or celestial kingdom" (*Gospel Principles*, chapter 45).

Speaking of terrestrial beings, the revelations state: "These are they who receive of [Jesus Christ's] glory, but not of his fulness." So, is there a difference between what some inhabitants can enjoy and receive. See the next question.

How do we gain entrance into the city of New Jerusalem?

Michael Wilcox described it this way: "One enters the city through participation in the house of Israel. Baptism is the ordinance, the rebirth, that enables us to claim the blessings of membership in the family of Israel." Baptism puts us on a narrow path toward the city of God. We must be worthy of and instructed in the ordinances of the temple. We must be endowed in the holy temple. Wilcox adds, "When we complete the last edifying moment in the endowment, we are in some measure enacting our final entrance through the gates of the holy city" (*Who Shall Be Able To Stand?: Finding Personal Meaning in the Book of Revelation*, 305–306; see also Revelation 21:12–13, 27 and 2 Nephi 31:9, 18). Will some not choose this edifying moment and be content in the Savior's glory, but not His fulness? So then, will there be other places of gathering (cities) that will not be consider Zion or one of her stakes?

Will there be a distinct wall around the New Jerusalem and other stakes (cities) of Zion?

Some remarks by Brigham Young suggest this. Others mention gates to the city. If there are gates, we may assume there are walls. Isaiah said that the walls would be known as "salvation" and the gates "praise" (Isaiah 60:18). The New Jerusalem Scroll (a very fragmented document in the collection of the Dead Sea Scrolls) indicates the city is laid out in the shape of a rectangle. The record also indicates that there are twelve gates with the sons of Jacob (Twelve tribes of Israel) each representing a gates name. This also seems to accord with John the Beloved's account in Revelation 21 (except the city in John's account is perfectly squared. We know the "holy Jerusalem" city John saw coming "out of heaven from God" would have walls and gates and angels at those gates prohibiting entrance to "anything that defileth" (see Revelation 21:9–27).

How will the Lord be a defense for "mount Zion"?

Isaiah foresaw the Lord would extend heavenly help collectively, but also individually to those assembled in mount Zion. See Isaiah 4:5–6 (2 Nephi 14:5–6).

Will there be an increase in the birthrate in New Jerusalem?

If Zion, the New Jerusalem, is the antithesis of today's trends, we may assume a very strong YES here. See also D&C 45:58. It says the inhabitants "will multiply and wax strong" as their children continue to "grow up without sin unto salvation." I also suggest reading 4 Nephi 1:10 in context.

Will the city of New Jerusalem be larger than the other cities (stakes of Zion) to be established?

As a world capital for the Savior's millennial reign, we may suppose that the New Jerusalem will be distinct in some ways. Joseph Smith's community concept of Zion had multiple communities being established with each community between 15,000–20,000 people. Was this a stake of Zion idea? To answer these question in four words: I have no idea.

Is it true that the New Jerusalem will be a library and reservoir of ancient records?

Orson Pratt did matter-of-factly declare that "the day should come for them (the records of the Nephites) to be transferred to the sacred temple of Zion." (*Millennial Star*, July 7, 1866.) Consider the records like the brass plates and those held by the lost tribes to return with the words of their prophets. Can you imagine having access to ancient records? Will there be a publication of these records? Alma told Helaman that the plates of brass would be preserved by the hand of the Lord until they should go forth to "every nation, kindred, tongue, and people" (see Alma 37:4). Time will tell.

What kind of knowledge will be disseminated from the New Jerusalem after the Lord comes and makes His abode there?

Ponder Doctrine and Covenants 101:32–34; 121:26–32. The bringing forth of all ancient records and records of heaven will make for exciting and wonderful reading. But also, being taught from resurrected personages will be deeply rewarding.

Will there be business establishments and exchanges, and infrastructure familiar to us presently?

Well, I can tell you this. If you want to know if you love all of God's children go into a Walmart on a Saturday at 1 p.m. If you can come out of the store with a smile on your face and not mumbling any bad words, you can say that you do possess enough love to dwell in New Jerusalem. Something must test the condition of our heart. All kidding aside, surely there will be exchanges of resources, items, and product. There will be transactions of some sort. How and what that looks like, I have no idea. For this question and the next three questions, it should be remembered that social experiences and services are very much dependent upon each other. The Kingdom of God will obviously stand in a position of strength when it comes to vital resources and services to allow people to continue in a state of existence. Other entities may offer services and resources, but we will not have a dependence upon them. If they fail, the void will be filled.

Will there be travel among stakes of Zion and the New Jerusalem and the Jerusalem of old?

We (I), sure hope so. Obviously, there may be time in the beginning of the buildup of the city that conflict and situations may not inhibit travel. But once the Lord subdues those troubles it seems reasonable to enjoy safe travel and interaction via communication, in a variety of ways, with other stakes/cities of Zion.

What will the architecture and building material be in the New Jerusalem?

The minerals and metals must be magnificent and not given to deterioration as we see in some of today's materials. As far as architecture, beats me. If the Lord gave variety to the earth for beauty and enjoyment, couldn't we expect such variety in buildings and homes in New Jerusalem? For the record, if there are split entry homes in New Jerusalem, I don't want one. We lived in one for twelve years. I've done my time.

Will we only eat food from gardens, plants, trees, and so on—food that we plant and harvest?

Surely eating such food will be part of the work and joy of our existence in Zion. But don't forget that when the resurrected Lord appeared to some disciples in Jerusalem, He was given and did eat broiled fish and honeycomb (see Luke 24:42–43). Does the Lord have a sweet tooth? Just asking. Chocolate deserves a place in the holy city. Just saying. The Lord eating after His resurrection indicates resurrected beings can eat some of what we eat. What about translated beings? Well, we'll see when Enoch and a host of others show up to join us in an assimilated New Jerusalem of grandeur. If they can't or don't, I'm sure they'll let us know.

Will there be sports in the New Jerusalem (asking for a friend)?

Well, I can say this—the Kansas City Chiefs Arrowhead Stadium and the Kansas City Royals Kauffman Stadium stand next to each other on a piece of land right in the middle of Jackson County. Just saying. Organized sports as we now know it? Hardly. But there seems to be some reasoning in the idea of sport and exercise being a worthwhile components of the New Jerusalem. To answer the question in four words: I have no idea.

Will there be other forms of entertainment in the New Jerusalem (asking for another friend)?

Why not? I addressed work, industry, and cleanliness in this book. Certainly a wide range of entertainment will complement a Zion society. The difference between now and then is the virtue, power, and purpose of the entertainment. Entertainment will reflect holiness, joy, and good sense. Speaking of sense, particularly senses, I believe acquiring godliness remarkably heightens our vision, hearing, touch, smell, and taste. Thus, bringing greater joy to the whole being. Are the senses we are given in mortality to serve a much higher purpose in the resurrection? We should expect wholesome activities, foods, recreation, and leisure that will be filtered by these heightened senses for experiencing greater joy.

As you can tell form the last three questions, I am digressing. I'll stop here.

Appendix B

Zion, the New Jerusalem, in the Old Testament

In chapter 4, you considered the references to Zion, the New Jerusalem, scattered throughout the Doctrine and Covenants. I thought it would be helpful to provide Old Testament references.

Recall that Joseph Smith stated: "The building up of Zion is a cause that has interested the people of God in every age; it is a theme upon which prophets, priests, and kings have dwelt with peculiar delight; they have looked forward with joyful anticipation to the day in which we lived; and fired with heavenly and joyful anticipations they have sung, and wrote, and prophesied of this our day;—but they died without the sight" ("History, 1838–1856, volume C-1 [2 November 1838–31 July 1842]," 1327, *The Joseph Smith Papers*, accessed October 15, 2021, https://www.josephsmithpapers.org/paper-summary/history-1838-1856-volume-c-1-2-november-1838-31-july-1842/501.) The references on the following pages are some of those songs, writings, and prophecies.

ZION, THE NEW JERUSALEM, IN THE OLD TESTAMENT	
Reference	**Synopsis/Text of Scripture**
Psalm 2:6	"Yet I have set ["anointed" in Hebrew] my king upon my holy hill of Zion."
Psalm 9:11	"Sing praises to the Lord, which dwelleth in Zion: declare among the people his doings." Jesus Christ told the Nephites that He would reign in Zion (3 Nephi 21:25). It will be a throne of perfect judgment. He will be a refuge for the oppressed and when troubles are poured out upon the wicked (the proceeding verses in Psalm 9:7–10).
Psalm 14:7	"Oh that the salvation of Israel were come out of Zion! When the Lord bringeth back the captivity of his people." The Lord will gather scattered Israel. They will rejoice and find gladness in their temporal and spiritual salvation.
Psalm 48:1–3, 10–14	Everything about Zion will exuberate the excellence and virtue of the Lord. "Great is the Lord, and greatly to be praised in the city of our God, in the mountain of his holiness. Beautiful for situation, the joy of the whole earth, is mount Zion, on the sides of the north, the city of the great King. God is known in her palaces for a refuge. . . . "According to thy name, O God, so is thy praise unto the ends of the earth: thy right hand is full of righteousness. Let mount Zion rejoice, let the daughters of Judah be glad, because of thy judgments. Walk about Zion, and go round about her: tell the towers thereof. Mark ye well her bulwarks, consider her palaces; that ye may tell it to the generation following. For this God is our God for ever and ever: he will be our guide even unto death."

Psalm 50:2–6	Jesus Christ will be a righteous judge who will gather saints who honor their covenants. "Out of Zion, the perfection of beauty, God hath shined. Our God shall come, and shall not keep silence: a fire shall devour before him, and it shall be very tempestuous round about him. "He shall call to the heavens from above, and to the earth, that he may judge his people. *Gather my saints together unto me; those that have made a covenant with me by sacrifice.* And the heavens shall declare his righteousness: for God is judge himself" (emphasis added).
Psalm 87:1–3, 5–7	"His foundation is in the holy mountains. The Lord loveth the gates of Zion more than all the dwellings of Jacob. Glorious things are spoken of thee, O city of God . . . . "And of Zion it shall be said, This and that man was born in her: and the highest himself shall establish her. The Lord shall count, when he writeth up the people, that this man was born there . . . As well the singers as the players on instruments shall be there: *all my springs are in thee.*" The concept of *springs* means sources of joy and happiness.

Psalm 102:12–22	"But thou, O Lord, shalt endure forever; and thy remembrance unto all generations. Thou shalt arise, and have mercy upon Zion: for the time to favour her, yea, the set time, is come. For thy servants take pleasure in her stones, and favour the dust thereof. So the heathen shall fear the name of the Lord, and all the kings of the earth thy glory. "When the Lord shall build up Zion, he shall appear in his glory. He will regard the prayer of the destitute, and not despise their prayer. This shall be written for the generation to come: and the people which shall be created shall praise the Lord. For he hath looked down from the height of his sanctuary; from heaven did the Lord behold the earth; To hear the groaning of the prisoner; to loose those that are appointed to death; To declare the name of the Lord in Zion, and his praise in Jerusalem; When the people are gathered together, and the kingdoms, to serve the Lord." Once again, we see distinctions of Zion and Jerusalem of old. We see that Zion will be the antithesis of the crumbling world. The prayers of the destitute and poor shall be addressed by the Lord. People we proclaim the divinity of Jesus Christ.
Psalm 132:13–16	"For the Lord hath chosen Zion; he hath desired it for his habitation. This is my rest for ever: here will I dwell; for I have desired it. I will abundantly bless her provision: I will satisfy her poor with bread. I will also clothe her priests with salvation: and her saints shall shout aloud for joy." The Lord told the Nephites He would dwell "in the midst" of the people of Zion (see 3 Nephi 21:25).
Isaiah 1:26–27	"And I will restore thy judges as at the first, and thy counsellors as at the beginning: afterward thou shalt be called, The city of righteousness, the faithful city. Zion shall be redeemed with judgment, and her converts with righteousness." All tyrannical and misguided governments of men will fail. They will come to an end. The Lord's judgments upon them will allow Zion to flourish."

Isaiah 2:3 (Micah 4:2)	"For out of Zion shall go forth the law, and the word of the Lord from Jerusalem." The distinction of the these two capital cities is highlighted. The sovereignty of Zion shall influence the whole world. The laws of Jesus Christ will be set forth. We will have no laws, but His laws, when He comes. Cross reference Doctrine and Covenants 38:21–22.
Isaiah 4:3–6	This shall occur as a cleansing begins in the early days of the Millennium. "And it shall come to pass, that he that is left in Zion, and he that remaineth in Jerusalem, shall be called holy, even every one that is written among the living in Jerusalem: When the Lord shall have washed away the filth of the daughters of Zion, and shall have purged the blood of Jerusalem from the midst thereof by the spirit of judgment, and by the spirit of burning. "And the Lord will create upon every dwelling place of mount Zion, and upon her assemblies, a cloud and smoke by day, and the shining of a flaming fire by night: for upon all the glory shall be a defence. And there shall be a tabernacle for a shadow in the daytime from the heat, and for a place of refuge, and for a covert from storm and from rain."
Isaiah 14:32	As Babylon falls, they will seek answers from the Lord's chosen people. Isaiah foresaw: "What shall one then answer the messengers of the nation? That *the Lord hath founded Zion*, and the poor of his people shall trust in it."
Isaiah 24:23	The distinction of Jerusalem and Zion, the New Jerusalem, are once again stated. They shall be important places of the Lord's millennial reign. "Then the moon shall be confounded, and the sun ashamed, when the Lord of hosts shall reign in mount Zion, and in Jerusalem, and before his ancients gloriously."

Isaiah 33:20	"Look upon Zion, the city of our solemnities: thine eyes shall see Jerusalem a quiet habitation, a tabernacle that shall not be taken down; not one of the stakes thereof shall ever be removed, neither shall any of the cords thereof be broken." The Lord's promises about Zion, Jerusalem, and their stakes will be fulfilled.
Isaiah 35:10	"And the ransomed of the Lord shall return, and come to Zion with songs and everlasting joy upon their heads: they shall obtain joy and gladness, and sorrow and sighing shall flee away." Difficult days will proceed Zion's triumph, but individuals will receive the Lord's blessings.
Isaiah 46:13	"I bring near my righteousness; it shall not be far off, and my salvation shall not tarry: and I will place salvation in Zion for Israel my glory." This, I believe alludes to both temporal and spiritual salvation.
Isaiah 51:3	"For the Lord shall comfort Zion: he will comfort all her waste places; and he will make her wilderness like Eden, and her desert like the garden of the Lord; joy and gladness shall be found therein, thanksgiving, and the voice of melody." There will be a remarkable reclamation of the region Zion will occupy—indeed eventually the whole earth. The Lord will influence and sustain all efforts and the people shall help Him bring about the renewal of the land.
Isaiah 52:1	"Awake, awake; put on thy strength, O Zion; put on thy beautiful garments, O Jerusalem, the holy city: for henceforth there shall no more come into thee the uncircumcised and the unclean." See also Doctrine and Covenants 113:7–8.

Isaiah 59:20	"And the Redeemer shall come to Zion, and unto them that turn from transgression in Jacob, saith the Lord." The Lord will give attention to the people at large, but the beauty of who He is allows each of us to know Him personally. He allows each of us one-on-one time as we turn from sin and ignorance (see D&C 113:9–10).
Isaiah 61:3–4	"To appoint unto them that mourn in Zion, to give unto them beauty for ashes, the oil of joy for mourning, the garment of praise for the spirit of heaviness; that they might be called trees of righteousness, the planting of the Lord, that he might be glorified. And they shall build the old wastes, they shall raise up the former desolations, and they shall repair the waste cities, the desolations of many generations." Again, we have a clear indication that desolation (self-inflicted and from the Lord's judgments) will occur. But Zion will have an answer and a great momentum of restoration and cleansing.

Isaiah 62:1–5, 12	As Zion begins to be established in the last days the Lord has promised: "For Zion's sake will I not hold my peace, and for Jerusalem's sake I will not rest, until the righteousness thereof go forth as brightness, and the salvation thereof as a lamp that burneth. And the Gentiles shall see thy righteousness, and all kings thy glory: and thou shalt be called by a new name, which the mouth of the Lord shall name. "Thou shalt also be a crown of glory in the hand of the Lord, and a royal diadem in the hand of thy God. Thou shalt no more be termed Forsaken; neither shall thy land any more be termed Desolate: but thou shalt be called Hephzi-bah [my desire is in her], and thy land Beulah [married wife]: for the Lord delighteth in thee, and thy land shall be married. For as a young man marrieth a virgin, so shall thy sons marry thee: and as the bridegroom rejoiceth over the bride, so shall thy God rejoice over thee. "And they shall call them, The holy people, The redeemed of the Lord: and thou shalt be called, Sought out, A city not forsaken."
Jeremiah 3:14	"Turn, O backsliding children, saith the Lord; for I am married unto you: and I will take you one of a city, and two of a family, and I will bring you to Zion." I do not think this means exactly as it sounds. Rather, the Lord will bring those from all over, but the numbers may be uniquely surprising. Inheritances will seem like very few amongst the heavily populated cities and large families. In truth, enormous faithful families will receive their deserved inheritance.
Jeremiah 31:6	Sometime in the last days this will occur: "For there shall be a day, that the watchmen upon the mount Ephraim shall cry, Arise ye, and let us go up to Zion unto the Lord our God." Hasten the day. This will be a crucial point in the build up of New Jerusalem.

Joel 2:32	"And it shall come to pass, that whosoever shall call on the name of the Lord shall be delivered: for in mount Zion and in Jerusalem shall be deliverance, as the Lord hath said, and in the remnant whom the Lord shall call." Consider Isaiah 26:20–21. The Lord is a faithful deliverer.
Joel 3:16	"The Lord also shall roar out of Zion, and utter his voice from Jerusalem; and the heavens and the earth shall shake: but the Lord will be the hope of his people, and the strength of the children of Israel." The Millennium is His reign. The strength of His voice and His sovereignty will crash down upon some stubborn individuals clamoring for power. People will trust in Him and not little pharaoh's sitting upon stools.
Micah 4:7, 11–13	There's an interesting line in this verse. Micah foresaw that dispersed Israel would help establish a strong nation in a far location unknown to him. Also, this nation would eventually provide resources for the establishment of Zion. "And I will make her that halted a remnant, and her that was cast far off a strong nation: and the Lord shall reign over them in mount Zion from henceforth, even for ever. "Now also many nations are gathered against thee, that say, Let her be defiled, and let our eye look upon Zion. But they know not the thoughts of the Lord, neither understand they his counsel: for he shall gather them as the sheaves into the floor. Arise and thresh, O daughter of Zion: for I will make thine horn iron, and I will make thy hoofs brass: and thou shalt beat in pieces many people: and I will consecrate their gain unto the Lord, and their substance unto the Lord of the whole earth."

Zephaniah 3:16	"In that day [the last days near the Second Coming] it shall be said to Jerusalem, Fear thou not: and to Zion, Let not thine hands be slack." There will be plenty to do in Zion, the New Jerusalem. Everyone will have an appointed labor. Cross reference Doctrine and Covenants 68:30.

– Notes –

– Notes –

About the Author

Ryan C. Jenkins is the author of *The Assassination of Joseph Smith: Innocent Blood on the Banner of Liberty*. In this book on the New Jerusalem, he sets forth a central theme amplified by Joseph Smith—the gathering of a people who will establish and sustain a holy city. He presents seventeen topics associated with this holy city on the horizon. With some irony (or a lot), Ryan was born and lived among the bright lights and billboards of Las Vegas. Today, he and his wife, Melissa, reside in Columbia, Missouri. They recently began welcoming grandchildren into the world.